D1430058

HAUNTED
MEMORIES

Portraits of Women in the Holocaust

Lucille Eichengreen

PublishingWorks, Inc.

2011

PublishingWorks, Inc.,
151 Epping Road
Exeter, NH 03833
603-778-9883

For Sales and Orders:
1 603-772-7200
Distributed to the trade by PGW

Designed by: Anna Pearlman

LCCN: 2010912639
ISBN-13: 978-1-935557-67-8

HAUNTED MEMORIES

Portraits of Women in the Holocaust

Lucille Eichengreen

For Barry, Martin and Michelle

ACKNOWLEDGMENTS

My thanks and appreciation to my friends for their support and encouragement; to my agent and editors for their helpful suggestions and guidance; my thoughts to the women who had crossed my path years ago, but not last, to my children for their constant love.

"Scars remind us where we have been—
only the dead can forgive . . ."

Contents

Introduction

I beg you
do something
learn a dance step
something to justify your existence
something that gives you the right
to be dressed in your skin in your body hair
learn to walk and to laugh
because it would be too senseless
after all
for so many to have died
while you live
doing nothing with your life.

—Charlotte Delbo, *Useless Knowledge*

Like Lucille Eichengreen, Charlotte Delbo, the author of *Useless Knowledge*, is a survivor of Auschwitz. Also like Eichengreen, Delbo waited many years before publishing her memoir, exhorting readers to appreciate life, to live it to the fullest, if only in vicarious recognition of all the women who could not dance or walk or laugh. It was with a similar sense of mission that Lucille wrote her three books: *From Ashes to Life: My Memories of the Holocaust*; *Rumkowski and the Orphans of Lodz*; and this, her most current work, *Haunted Memories: Women in the Holocaust.*

Lucille Eichengreen began writing in her sixties, fifty years after the fact, because "it is too painful to go back. It still is." There were other reasons she waited so long, though maybe not as personal. First, biographies by women of the Holocaust were not popular fifty years ago. Only men were considered credible witnesses. Secondly, publishers did not see Holocaust books as "money makers." So, with only notes but no plans to write, she told her stories to her children when they were old enough to understand. Thus, she kept the stories alive.

It was a poet from the San Francisco Bay Area who encouraged Lucille to write her memories. She began modestly, writing poems, some of which were translated and published in Israel and Germany. When she retired from work in the 1980s, she decided it was time to clean up the Holocaust material. "Some of the material," she admits, "I found difficult to put down on paper . . . Like, for instance, what happened to my sister. I just, just couldn't put this in writing. It was that difficult."

For several years, Lucille worked on her first book with her friend Professor Harriet Hyman Chamberlain, writing and revising chapters as often as ten times. Then, with the aid of an agent, she found a publisher, Mercury House. Once the manuscript was accepted, they sent it to an accomplished editor. "However," she explains, "the editor wanted to make a novel out of it. He wanted it to be beautiful, smooth and polished. But the life I was writing about wasn't polished. I wanted it to be harsh and abrupt." (Quoted in a thesis by Catherine Bernard, page 34.) She changed editors, and the book, *From Ashes to Life, My Memories of the Holocaust*, was finally published in 1994.

Lucille's story is indeed harsh. After being taken from her comfortable family of Polish descent, she endured every aspect of Nazi racial hatred, first in her hometown of Hamburg, then successively in the Lodz Ghetto, Auschwitz, Neuengamme and Bergen-Belsen. She survived every kind of degradation from slave labor to abject starvation. She irretrievably lost her family and her home, but never her human spirit. After the liberation, she helped the Allied troops identify perpetrators. She immigrated to the United States of America, married, raised a family, and built a successful business career.

It is through her book that I came to know Lucille personally. As a scholar and teacher of the Holocaust, and as the co-editor of a recently published Holocaust-related memoir, I have read dozens and dozens of such books. Yet, I consistently choose *From Ashes to Life* to teach to my students. Lucille's lucid writing style, her clear-eyed vision, the poignancy of her story, and the way it so effectively illustrates the systematic cruelty of Nazis toward Jews make her book more than an effective teaching tool. Cynthia Ozick, author of *The Shawl*, has said of Lucille's book, "It crashes in on the reader with absolute authenticity; one knows instantly that nothing here is 'made up,' everything has been seen, smelled, endured, suffered . . . I am harrowed by it . . . The truth-telling, the economy, the spare moral cry of it."

In the year 2006, Lucille published her second memoir, *Rumkowski and the Orphans of Lodz*. I was absolutely staggered by this book. It recounts the perversion and sexual abuse women and children suffered at the hands of Chaim Rumkowski, the Nazi-appointed Jewish Elder of the Lodz Ghetto. *Rumkowski and the Orphans of Lodz* is an incredibly important contribution to the study of how the women were treated during the Holocaust.

Lucille Eichengreen was born Cecilia Landau in Hamburg, Germany, on February 1, 1925. Before her birth, her parents had emigrated from Poland to Hamburg seeking economic opportunities as well as to escape the Polish pogroms. Lucille remembers a happy and secure family life with music lessons, Jewish school days and summer vacations. Martin Buber, the renowned Jewish philosopher, visited the book-lined study where

Lucille's father held conversations on philosophical and political topics.

Then, on January 1933, two days before Lucille's eighth birthday, Hitler came into power. In the opening chapter of *From Ashes to Life*, aptly entitled "Foreboding," Lucille recalls that time and how she tried to understand the word "anti-Semitism" used by her elders. She recalls the increasing instances of name-calling by former playmates, her mounting fears—resulting in a deteriorating performance at school—and the family's forced removal from their apartment.

In October 1938, her beloved father was arrested and deported to Poland. He returned in May 1939 only to be arrested again in September and sent to Dachau, where he died early in 1941.

That same year, in August, the Nazis deported Lucille, her mother Sala, and her younger sister Karin to the Lodz Ghetto. The three years she spent in Lodz were, in many ways, the most difficult of her twelve-year Holocaust experience. Her mother died of starvation in the ghetto eighteen months after the death of her father. Thus, at the age of seventeen, Lucille and her sister were orphans. Sala had exhorted Lucille to take care of Karin, but she watched helplessly as Karin was "sent east." Now, she was totally alone.

Nonetheless, the predatory attention she received from Chaim Rumkowski was far from welcome. Rumkowski held absolute control over the Jews imprisoned in the ghetto. If he added one's name to a deportation list, it was a virtual death sentence. The Nazis, who had appointed him, were certainly not interested in appeals from the Jews who suffered from his demands. Thus, the powers he held to command sexual favors were almost unlimited.

Other victims' testimonies, those she met in the Lodz Ghetto as well as those whom she sought out after the Holocaust, helped to validate her own experience and to document just how widespread Rumkowski's crimes were. As director of the orphanage in Lodz before the war, Rumkowski habitually abused the boys and girls in his care. As the Elder of the Lodz Ghetto, he exacted sexual favors in exchange for food coupons, work assignments, and living quarters. Lucille recalls several encounters with the man in her second book, *Rumkowski and the Orphans of Lodz*. Her descriptions are graphic and deeply disturbing.

In August 1944, the Lodz Ghetto was liquidated. Lucille was deported to Auschwitz. She had never heard of Auschwitz until her arrival and was unaware of what was being done there. Her youth may have saved her from the worst. Within weeks, the Nazis sent her to a work camp in her hometown of Hamburg to clean up the bomb damage at the harbor.

After transferring to another work camp, she helped to build concrete houses for Germans who had been bombed out of their homes. In March 1945, she was again transferred, this time to Bergen-Belsen, from which she was liberated on April 15, 1945. From there, Lucille's story moves to her life in a displaced persons camp, her work with the British Army identifying Holocaust perpetrators, her escape to France, and on to America, where she met her husband, Dan Eichengreen.

As compelling as Lucille's memoirs about the Holocaust may be, their significance goes beyond her personal experience.

The 1983 Conference on Women Surviving the Holocaust held at Stern College in New York City is commonly cited as the earliest attention paid to women of the Holocaust. Oddly, women survivors, even those who attended the conference, tend to resist a gendered analysis of their experience. Efforts to theorize the Shoah, its causes and how its effects differed for men and for women are frequently seen by survivors as so much intellectual posturing. Their pain-filled and desperate memories do not easily yield to theorizing and abstraction.

Lucille Eichengreen is something of an exception to this generalization. Although some believe that to focus on gender is to trivialize the Holocaust by emphasizing sexism over anti-Semitism, Lucille believes that we must consider gender in order to fully understand the Holocaust. In *Rumkowski and the Orphans of Lodz*, she viscerally describes the ways in which a female's experience was different from a male's: indeed, the sexual abuse women endured at the hands of Rumkowski was frequent and horrifying. Although other survivors have told of sexual abuses, they focus on what happened to others, not themselves. A sense of privacy, or shame, may be the reason behind this reticence, as well as society's tendency to "blame the victim."

Eichengreen has been more than courageous in describing her own victimization. Writing *Rumkowski and the Orphans of Lodz* required a double dose of courage: revealing the depredations of a fellow Jew and revealing her own humiliation and victimization.

Rumkowski and the Orphans of Lodz challenges what some have called "the master narrative of the Holocaust," namely, the emphasis on the male experience and the assumption that women's experiences can be generalized from the male's. Yet the publication of solid new studies of women and the Holocaust indicate a growing acceptance of a gender approach. Yes, gender did diversely effect how men and women experienced the Holocaust. At last, the truism spoken by Joan Ringelheim at the 1983 conference is being recognized. If half of the population that went through the Holocaust was female, "how, in the name of the Holocaust and in the name of all the people who were in it, can we not talk about women?" It is this task that Lucille Eichengreen, with so many other women survivors and scholars, has taken on.

Lucille Eichengreen has received well-deserved recognition for her books. Her work, some of which has been translated into German, appears in a number of anthologies. Kirkus Review praises *From Ashes to Life* as "a most eloquent Holocaust memoir, distinguished by symmetry of storytelling and theme . . . a skillful, dramatic, unsentimental blend of introspections and action." In 1994, *From Ashes to Life* was chosen from among fifteen hundred candidates by the *School Library Journal* as one of thirteen "Best Adult Books for Young Adults." Of *Rumkowski and the Orphans of Lodz, Publisher's Weekly* states: "Eichengreen offers what appears to be an insurmountable case again Rumkowski . . . The sexual abuse detailed here in spare, chilling prose is just the most egregious of the material and emotional hardships of ghetto life that made human decency virtually impossible. The author cogently describes the exploitation and deceit that infested the intimate relationships in the ghetto."

I have been privileged to work as a reviewer of early drafts of *Haunted Memories*. I felt especially honored because I am convinced that this book is an invaluable resource for students and scholars of the Holocaust. Each of over a dozen chapters recounts the story of a different woman who was victimized amid the horrors of the Third Reich. Lucille tells the women's stories as she recollects them: a mother watching a child die; a sympathetic Nazi guard; a dangerous lesbian relationship; a couple shunned by their fellow Jews for being Christian converts; a dysfunctional sister-and-brother relationship; a brave woman doctor in Auschwitz; a fearless slave laborer who resisted to her death. Lucille tells, too, in spare profoundly affecting prose, of Sala, her own mother, as she lay dying in the ghetto.

Eichengreen has many gifts as a writer: she seizes upon the kernel, the essence, and without preaching lets it unfold to reveal both the human experience and the moral issues within. Students often tell me that once they begin reading her books, they stay up all night to finish them. What is more, Lucille writes with the authority of a survivor, an authority that will be left solely to the printed page and documentary films as the ranks of survivors thin dramatically each year. She is a survivor and she is willing to tell her story. With her first two books, and now this latest one, Lucille shares her "haunted memories" and shapes them into lessons for the world.

—Elisabeth Baer

Preface

Surviving the Lodz Ghetto, Auschwitz, Neuengamme and Bergen-Belsen was just short of a miracle. I was eight years old and living in Hamburg, Germany, when Hitler seized power. I was twenty when the war came to an end. Twelve long years of horror, deprivation, dehumanization and hunger had taken their toll on all of the women, their husbands and most of all on their children.

Statistics about the number of imprisoned men and women are not accurate and are not readily available, because records are incomplete. Historians are not entirely sure how many people were in captivity at the beginning of the war, or when Hitler seized power after 1933 or even in 1940 or 1941. Although we do know the total number of survivors, these numbers are not broken down into men and women, and are also not totally reliable.

Most memoirs about the Holocaust—at least until about fifteen years ago—were written by male survivors. Perhaps women were reluctant to write or talk about the past. Or, it may be that most publishers did not trust the validity of a woman's recall. Women were considered unreliable, lacking objectivity or truthfulness. But now, thanks to gender studies and woman awareness, publishers have come to realize that our experiences are equally valid, equally important, and also very different in many aspects from the experiences of men.

Looking back, both men and women were subjected to various forms of sexual abuse. Submitting to sex in the camps often meant additional food. Do we condemn these people? Of course not! Driven to both mental and physical limits, as well as bartered sex, anything was and is possible. In female camps there were rapes, as well as sexual favors bartered for a slice of bread or a potato. We knew, we saw, and we heard, but we did not talk about it. We were helpless and thus silent.

Women in Europe during the thirties and even beyond were second-class citizens. We worked as nurses, secretaries, teachers and homemakers, but we were never in charge of an office, a factory, or of a group of workers.

However, in the Lodz Ghetto during the period of 1940 to 1944, there was a sudden and drastic change. For just about the first time, women were in charge of factories, offices, workers' kitchens, and every other area of ghetto life. These women were capable, intelligent, hard-working and ambitious. They wanted to survive. They wanted power to at least determine a part of their lives under conditions that were far from normal. And they succeeded. Even the men guardedly and grudgingly admitted that the women in managerial positions were effective, accomplished and working at the peak of human ability.

Women who wielded power in the ghetto had their protégés just like men. But their protégés were generally male. These powerful women seldom reached out or helped other women. I experienced this when I was just sixteen years old and applied for jobs in various factories. Any kind of a job. The women did not even accord me the time to listen to my pleas. The male bosses, on the other hand, were more than willing to give me employment. Their only question was, "What are you willing to give me in return?" Naive and uncomprehending, I replied, "I have no money, no jewelry, in fact nothing of value." The harsh laughter that followed left me stunned. I failed to understand. It took a year of ghetto life to learn the facts of life; if you asked for a favor, you had to be willing to submit to sex. It was as simple as that.

There were exceptions—not many, but I was one of the fortunate ones. I did find a job without having to compromise myself.

Even within the ghetto, our own people, from Rumkowski to a boss in the sheet-metal shop, considered sex a commodity to be traded. But not everybody was willing to trade. Some of us preferred to starve.

Don't misunderstand me. Not all friendships or alliances were business arrangements based on an exchange: food for services rendered. There were true love stories. There was commitment and devotion. Some of these loves survived separation and war and lasted for years beyond liberation.

Women formed friendships that lasted long beyond the war. They supported each other and often expressed a closeness and a devotion not even seen in families. Yes, we had enemies from within as well. Other women betrayed us, denounced us, cheated us and stole our food or our shoes. In the concentration camps, from Auschwitz to Neuengamme to Bergen-Belsen, it was pretty much the same. We relied on each other, we helped each other and we despaired together.

Jewish women in charge in the various concentration camps were *Kapos*, or camp police. These Kapos and the camp elders were appointed by the Germans. They followed German orders and we could accept that. However, there were those who went beyond orders, who caused much physical pain, gave inhuman beatings as well as emotional anguish. But they did not live long after the war; some were arrested and committed suicide. Others were killed or murdered. It was never clear who had killed them, and we did not ask.

The German attitude toward Jewish women was a strange mix of cruelty and restraint. They made us work hard, they beat us, they starved us, they shot us. We endured rain and snow dressed in rags. They exploited us beyond endurance. Yet, compared to the Jewish men, our lot was easy. The men were beaten, starved and made to work incredibly hard, often beyond human strength, carrying heavy loads and performing inhuman labor in underground mines, factories and stone quarries.

Drawing a comparison now, it seems that the Germans still had the old-fashioned work ethic in mind and lived by it: women were the weaker sex, and while they had to work hard, compared to the work demanded and expected of men, less was expected of women. Yet, I recall slave labor: cleaning up bomb damage with my bare hands in rain and snow. I recall infected hands. I recall constant colds and tuberculosis and the never-ending beatings and painful hunger. I recall an attempted rape by an SS man, when only a torn, salvaged rag saved me.

Then there were the women of the SS. For them too, and probably for the first time, they found themselves in positions of total control and authority. Frequently their cruelty and vindictiveness exceeded that of the male SS. They had to prove that they could handle what they called "a man's job." A Jewish woman to them was a useless twig, a piece of wood to be broken, destroyed, and discarded. They rarely associated with each other. Their friendships were limited to the SS men. I had expected some compassion from another woman, even an SS member. But only once did I experience a glimmer of compassion; as a rule the contrary was true.

Sixty-five years later, and we just now begin to remember and become aware of the experience of women in the Holocaust. It has taken a long time. Some of us survived. Many did not. We are old now and will soon be gone. But we cannot forget the past.

PART 1:

Hamburg Before the War

To the undiscerning eye, Hamburg is indeed a beautiful city, but to those of us who know what its people can—and do—harbor in their hearts, it can never seem beautiful.

The events that began in 1933 revealed the darker side of that city's nature and the lengths to which it could allow intolerance. The persecution of Jews became increasingly pronounced. At first, Jewish children had to attend special schools; later on, they were not allowed to go to school at all. Jewish teachers were no longer permitted to teach in state schools and universities. Jewish lawyers were no longer admitted to the bar, and Jewish businesses were boycotted. After Kristallnacht in November 1938, it should have been obvious to young and old alike that we Jews had a dismal future awaiting us, and I contend that the world should have opened its doors to us. But the nations of the world adhered to quotas and waiting lists, although some of the quotas and lists were not even completely fulfilled.

Those who remained in Hamburg, with few exceptions, perished.

Sala

"Let me tell you now about my life . . . I know I have little time left."Those were Sala's whispered words to me in the Lodz Ghetto in the summer of 1942. I sat down on the hard cot, which was our bed now, and waited. Never before had she talked much about her past but she must have known, as did I, that she was at death's door, that her days were numbered. Fragments I had heard as a child, but I knew few details.

The room was stuffy, the windows were closed, and the German who was downstairs stood guard behind the barbed wire fence. I was aware of the sound of his boots marching back and forth. Sala hesitantly began, and I forced myself to concentrate on her words.

"I was the youngest of eight surviving children of Chaim Elie and Ruchli Baumwollspinner. My mother's maiden name was Brudner. I was born in 1892 in Sambor, Poland. I lived with my parents, brothers and sisters and we were a close, caring family. When I was old enough, I was sent to school in Llow, learning Polish and German.

During the week I lived with a cousin since the commute to Sambor was too long. But my father picked me up every Friday in a horse-drawn buggy and took me home for Saturday and Sunday."

Sala's breathing was labored and heavy. I listened, wanting nothing more than to hear the end of her story. I cried quietly. I thought I saw a tear escaping her closed eyes too, running down her wrinkled cheek. She continued.

"The First World War from 1914 to 1918 was relatively painless for us; we grew our own vegetables and potatoes and owned the town's grocery store. The local peasants came daily, buying and selling goods, but there was always a hint of anti-Semitism in their remarks. During my time in Poland we were still considered part of the Austro-Hungarian empire.

"At war's end in 1918, I was twenty-six years old, and after I had finished school had learned to make and decorate ladies' hats. In those days this was an acceptable trade for a woman. In spite of being a dark-haired, slim beauty, not a single suitor had asked for my hand in marriage. My parents were worried. In 1919 my mother finally decided to send me to Cottbus [Germany], where my oldest brother, his wife and four children lived. He and his brother-in-law, Nathan, had established a wine import-export business. The firm had prospered and employed six traveling salesmen, among them my younger brother, Sig, and his friend Beno."

I held Sala's hand, hoping she would fall asleep. But she continued.

"Both Sig and Beno had served in the Austrian Army. Beno had been wounded, and they were now impatient to settle down to a normal life. Beno and I met in Cottbus, in Joseph's house. We saw each other often, fell in love and decided to marry. The family approved. Beno was good-looking, industrious, and there was nothing he could not do once he had set his mind to it. We married, and life for both of us changed drastically. We took a first step and moved to Hamburg and my brother Sig joined us. It was not an easy decision. We established our own wine import-export business but had not figured in Germany's runaway inflation of 1922. Our business almost faltered, but I, without Beno's knowledge, pawned my entire silverware to keep the business afloat."

Sala's eyes were closed and she fought exhaustion, but I could tell that she was determined to tell more. I was eager to hear her story, yet at the same time I wanted her to save her strength. I also sensed that her time was running out.

Sala struggled to say more: "The pawning of the silver was my first move of independence. That, and the cutting of the heavy dark braid I wore wound around my head. I had my hair cut in a fashionable 'bob,' short and elegant, and Beno was in a state of shock when he saw me! But he got used to it, especially since I deferred to him in all other matters. By the time Beno and I had our first daughter in 1925, I had retrieved my silverware and the business was doing well.

"Beno bought our first condominium in 1926 and we moved again in 1929 to a larger condo; three bedrooms, a living room, a study, kitchen and bath. Again it was Beno who made the decision and I never objected, nor did I voice an opinion. Our second daughter was born in 1930, and in 1935 Beno enrolled both girls in the Jewish Girls School in Hamburg.

"There was never a word of disagreement between us, and there was never any discord. I had been raised to leave all decisions to the men in the family, and specifically to my husband. It was just taken for granted in my time that this was the way it had to be. I never voiced objections or insisted on having my own way. I was content, naive and probably complacent.

"Each summer we spent wonderful vacations at various resorts in Germany and Denmark, and we returned to Poland from time to time to see my family. It was a good life. While the restrictions in Germany after 1933 bothered us, they did not personally affect us since we held Polish passports and hoped that we would be treated as foreign nationals." Sala paused. I could not stop crying. I hoped she would not notice.

"But suddenly in October 1938 all changed. Beno was picked up by the local police and transported to the German-Polish border together with 15,000 Polish nationals from throughout Germany. All of them were Jews. They were forced to walk across the border into Poland in spite of Polish resistance to let their own citizens enter."

Sala rested again. I held her hand in mine, and after a while she had gathered enough strength to continue.

"It was this sudden change in my life that propelled me into action. For the first time in my life I had to make all the decisions and my family depended on me. I was alone now and it was up to me to hold the family together. I made frequent visits to the Police Presidium requesting a permit for Beno's return. The Germans were not moved. In spring 1939 I decided to have all our belongings, the entire household, furniture, clothing, books, etc. packed by a freight forwarder. This was done under the watchful eye of German officials. Everything had to be packed in large containers, and these were supposed to be shipped to Beno's older brother in Haifa. He had wisely left Berlin in 1934 for Palestine. At that time he had pleaded with Beno to leave, but we were foolishly determined to stay." Sala's hand in mine was motionless and she did not seem to notice me, but somehow she knew I was listening, that I wanted to know, to hear and to understand.

"Painfully I waited until finally, in May 1939, Beno was granted permission for a temporary return of thirty days.

"I worked feverishly to obtain a certificate for Palestine or an affidavit from my brother in San Francisco, or if all would fail, then at least papers for Beno only. The children and I could always follow later, I thought. It had suddenly become urgent that we leave as

I realized the looming danger, the black clouds of doom, and the merciless attitude of the Germans. God did not hear my curses . . .

"I saw to it that Beno received several extensions to continue his stay in Germany. Then on September 1, 1939, Germany invaded Poland. The Gestapo arrested Beno at 6:00 A.M. I was heartbroken. But as soon as I found out that Beno had been sent to Concentration Camp Fuhlsbuettel, then to Sachsenhausen and finally Dachau, I wrote weekly letters to the Gestapo and followed them up with frequent visits to their headquarters at the Stadthaus offices. They threatened to arrest me, but I no longer cared. Nothing else mattered. Beno, only Beno . . ."

Sala closed her eyes for a short time, and I hoped she had fallen asleep. I was hurting. My feelings were raw and I silently wished she would not continue. But she rallied.

"Once, just once, I succeeded to have Beno brought to Gestapo headquarters, heavily guarded, sitting only four feet away. We could not touch, and we hardly spoke, only our eyes communicated in silence. Words were not needed. In fact, there were no words left.

"To no avail, I appeared again and again at the Gestapo offices. Even the officials at the Jewish Community Center only shrugged their shoulders—and I could not count on their help either.

"In February 1941, I saw two Germans in our kitchen and heard the dreaded German message: Beno Landau had died in Dachau. Onto the table the two Germans threw a cigar box filled with ashes from Dachau. My screams tore the silent air when I realized that Beno was gone from my life forever. At that moment I did not care to continue. But I had two children . . ." Sala paused again. Totally exhausted, she was barely able to continue, but she persisted. Her voice was low now, close to a whisper. I put my face next to hers, but she did not seem to be aware.

"Life had become unbearable. You, Karin and I were forced to move again and again, always into smaller quarters. The Germans assigned us one furnished room and then another, and we had to share a kitchen and a bath with eight or ten others. Our bank accounts had been blocked, and the money parceled out was not adequate to buy food and clothing. Life, such as it was, had become lonely—a living hell.

"October 1941 brought a letter advising us of a forced evacuation. Our destination was given as 'east.' We had to report within twenty-four hours. We were stuffed into sealed railroad cars, and two days later the train stopped. We were eleven hundred men, women and children, and had arrived in Lodz, Poland.

"I was sure that I would feel at home in Poland. I spoke the language, I knew the people, and the thought of a ghetto did not frighten me. I would somehow manage to make a home for myself and my two daughters. How wrong I was! I had not figured on or known about the lack of food, and the continuous hunger that would plague us. I sold many of my belongings: a blouse, a pair of shoes, even a coat, but they only brought temporary relief from hunger, and soon there was nothing left to sell. Winter was cruelly cold; there was no coal, no lumber with which to heat the room. Spring was beset by forced deportations of the elderly, the young and the unemployed, and I, once strong and determined, had now to rely on my children."

The room was quiet. I did not know if I should wait, if I should leave. Sala and I dozed off for a minute or two on her pillow. The pillow was wet, soaked with my tears, but she did not seem to notice.

"As you know," she continued, "I lost weight; my legs and feet became swollen, and I finally realized that I could fight no more."

Sala closed her eyes. I embraced her without a word. Tears ran freely down her shrunken face and my tears mingled with hers. She was breathing quietly now and drifted off. I lifted my head and watched her. She looked ancient, not like a fifty-year-old woman. There was so much I wanted to say, so much I wanted her to know, but the words were choking me.

Two days later, on a hot and humid day, July 13, 1942, she died in her sleep, without a word, without reproach or anger, and without regret. She had just given up.

Sala was my mother. I was alone and only seventeen years old and my little sister was twelve. A week later Karin and I dug a grave in the dry, parched soil of the ghetto cemetery in Marysin and buried her.

We could find no words, no tears and no prayer; there was not a soul to comfort us and we walked in silence the long road back into the ghetto. The midday sun was burning without mercy and I could only feel the silent, unspeakable pain.

Irmgard Schiller

For me, an eight-year-old child, the mood in Germany during the mid-thirties was turbulent, unpredictable, and insecure even at school. I attended a private Jewish girls' school where frequent references were made about the "new order" and to being a Jew surrounded by a hostile population. Confused and afraid, we asked ourselves: "Why are we afraid? Of whom are we afraid, and of what?" My parents did not show their feelings or voice the insecurity we felt. If they did, they spoke Polish, which we did not understand.

Between 1934 and 1935, my father and his business partner, who was his brother-in-law, bought several commercial and residential properties in Hamburg. Evidently, they had no fear that this might be a risky undertaking in Hitler's Germany, but rather looked forward to a secure economic future.

They hired Mr. Fritz Schiller, a licensed real estate broker and manager, to handle all business connected with tenants, vacancies, repairs, and other tenant matters.

Just once, my father took me along to Mr. Schiller's office downtown. He was a tall, good-looking man about my father's age, gracious and smiling, and kind to a timid girl. His secretary and assistant was a tall, blond woman in her thirties. There was an unsmiling curt way about her, and for a fleeting second I had the impression of her in a Nazi uniform. She never managed more than a "good morning," or "good-bye."

With the onset of the war in September 1939, my father was arrested and our lives changed overnight. My mother, sister, and I were compelled to live in a furnished room, moving from one location to another, at the whim of the German authorities. They called these locations Jewish Houses. We were strapped for money since all our accounts and property had been confiscated. We had to live on a small monthly allowance, which was sent to our bank from Berlin and did not cover the costs of food, rent, clothing and incidentals.

One day, Mother went to see Mr. Schiller. He listened patiently to her, and explained that he too had received instructions to forward all incoming monies to Berlin and found himself in a dangerous situation. But he was compassionate and kind enough to occasionally list a fake "repair" in his books and give my mother the cash. While his files were checked periodically by the German government, these small amounts that he managed to give us did not put him in jeopardy. It might have been a political risk, but it was no personal sacrifice.

Shortly after Father's arrest, Mr. Schiller married his secretary and my mother sent a small crystal wedding gift. His wife remained hostile and unpleasant whenever my mother visited the office, and I sensed that my mother was afraid Mrs. Schiller would report us to the authorities.

Mr. Schiller was drafted into the *Luftwaffe* (Air Force) about the same time that we received notification that my father had been murdered in Dachau in January 1941. In the fall of 1941, we were subjected to the wearing of a yellow star, which had to be sewn on all outer garments and had to be visible just below the left shoulder. Shortly thereafter, we received a notice for our deportation to "the east."

"Liberation"—if one can call it that—came on April 15, 1945, when the British Army stumbled upon Bergen-Belsen. I was the only member of my family who survived the horrors of four years in the ghetto of Lodz and subsequent deportation to the concentration camps: Auschwitz, Neuengamme, and Bergen-Belsen. Mother had died of hunger in the ghetto in July 1942, and my younger sister was deported in September of that year with thousands of other children who were destined to be murdered.

I started work almost immediately for the British and worked as an interpreter and translator. In summer, after the war in Germany had officially ended, I was eager and curious to return to Hamburg, if only for a look. My curiosity gave me no rest.

One of my superiors was a Lt. Jock, who came from Scotland, and was jolly and kind. He spoke with a Scottish brogue, and most of the time it was difficult for me to understand him. We often laughed when we failed to communicate what we had to say to one another.

Finally, in September 1945, Jock offered to drive me in his jeep to Hamburg. As he put it, "Let's have a look around." We stopped at the various rental properties that my father had bought in 1935, Alsenplatz, Scheideweg, and Gaertnerstrasse. I was fortunate enough to remember the addresses of Father's buildings. As it turned out, two of these buildings had "disappeared" into a huge crater, which covered the ground of the former buildings. They had been the target of Allied bombardment in 1943. The other two were still standing and fully occupied. I rang various bells, explained to the tenants who I was and gave them my name, and they in turn informed me that the German authorities had sold the properties and the new owners were now Aryans.

This scenario had not occurred to me and I was shocked speechless. The tenants offered Mr. Schiller's current telephone number and address. It was the location of an upper-middle-class neighborhood near the Isestrasse.

Jock started the jeep. I gave directions, and we found the building. We walked upstairs, located the name "Schiller," and rang the bell. The door was opened by Mrs. Schiller, and I recognized her instantly. The war years had not changed her and I believe that she knew who I was.

I started to talk slowly: "I am Cecilia Landau. Beno Landau's daughter. I would appreciate any information you can give me about my father's properties. I am the only surviving member of my immediate family and your help would be appreciated."

Mrs. Schiller looked at me; I felt cold hate. She did not reply, but she tried to close the door. Anticipating her move, Jock had his foot in the door and he did not budge. It was a comical tug of war, but Jock was considerably stronger than Mrs. Schiller. Eventually Mrs. Schiller had no choice but to open the door and to let us in. Her two boys were frightened and hiding behind her skirt. In a loud voice she ordered them out of the room. She did not offer us a chair, but Jock motioned, and he and I sat down. Sitting in her living room, I made another attempt.

"Mrs. Schiller, please let me have any information about my father's property," I pleaded.

She finally replied, "My husband is still in the Luftwaffe and has not as yet been released. I do not know his whereabouts, and I do not have any information." The reply was cold and I could feel the hatred that accompanied her words. I was thankful for Jock's presence.

I nodded my head. "But please give me the information you have accumulated during the past four years. After all, you worked for Mr. Schiller already before the war," I pleaded again.

"I have nothing at all," Mrs. Schiller curtly responded, and I translated what she said to Jock, who shook his head, removed his hand gun from its holster and slammed it on the table in front of him.

"You can give us the desired information or be taken to headquarters." Jock's words sounded ominous and Mrs. Schiller turned ashen. She seemed to have understood his English. The three of us looked at the gun on the table and slowly, reluctantly, Mrs. Schiller got up, walked over to a desk in the corner of the room, removed the file folders with my father's name on them, and gave me at least part of the information I needed. Her two boys peered through a slit in the door, and she motioned for them to leave.

When I looked at the files I saw that our name had been crossed out and another name substituted in its stead. Silently I went through the pages, disappointed and discouraged. I realized that there was nothing to be done now. I needed professional help to have the legal changes made. I stuttered my "thank you," Jock holstered his gun, and we left.

Fifteen years later, and with the help of several attorneys, court proceedings and appeals, the property was restored to the heirs of the original owners: to my cousin and to me. Eventually we sold the properties at a loss. Compensation for back rents was not even considered. In the meantime I had traveled to the United States in March of 1946.

It was not until 1990 that my husband and I decided to return to Germany at the invitation of the Hamburg Senate. Again, it was not an easy decision but we wanted to know and to see for ourselves what had changed in Germany and how its people had come to terms with the loss of the war.

Both Mrs. Schiller and her husband had died. Their son, Fritz, Jr., had taken over the business. During the past years we had occasionally corresponded, first on business matters, and later on a more personal level. Our relationship was polite—no more.

When Fritz heard about our visit to Hamburg, he offered to meet us at the airport, drive us to our hotel, and invited us to dinner at his home to meet his wife and children. Inevitably, the past entered our conversation. Fritz, Jr., surprised me with this recollection. "In 1945 your cousin from Sheffield, England, came to Hamburg accompanied by a British officer. My father was not with us at the time, but your cousin paid my mother a visit. To her last days, my mother never forgave him that he had the British officer put his hand gun on the table during the conversation. I was very young at that time, and hardly remember. But my mother spoke of the incident frequently, and was angry, insulted, and unforgiving until her death."

I was stunned. After I had gathered my thoughts, I responded:

"My cousin from Sheffield never came to Hamburg with a British officer. It was I who came to Hamburg in summer of 1945 with a British officer. Your mother refused to talk to me, to give me the requested information, and was very rude and hostile. And it was only then that the officer got impatient and put his gun on the table. But no threats were made. But miraculously the folders appeared and your mother reluctantly let me look at the files."

As soon as I had finished my statement I realized that I should not have told the truth but rather remained silent. I tried to be honest, but it was a foolish and useless gesture on my part. The son, like his mother before him, felt wronged and had no understanding of the past, or empathy of how Jews had been treated then—and now.

The room was filled with silence. Fritz Schiller looked at me. He seemed in a state of shock. His eyes were cold and filled with hate, and he reminded me of his late mother during my 1945 visit. Not a word was spoken. We finally got up, said our thank-you's and good-byes, and left.

I wrote a polite note from home. Fritz Schiller, Jr., still lives in Hamburg; in fact he had bought one of the buildings through another broker. But since the day of our visit, I never heard from him again.

In his eyes, and in the eyes of his mother, I had committed a terrible crime against a helpless, innocent woman who had refused to talk to a former client—a Jew.

Maria

My friend Rena was five years older than I. I really loved Rena. Her parents had befriended my mother in 1920 and her aunt had married my mother's brother. She had come from her home in Dresden to attend a preparatory course for students who wanted to settle in Palestine. The "home," called a "Kibbutz," a center for communal living, was located on Kielortallee 9, in Hamburg, not far from where my mother, sister and I lived in various furnished rooms from 1940 to 1941 while my father was still imprisoned in Dachau.

Rena had two older sisters who, together with their parents, had left Germany for Palestine. Her brother Adolph, whom we called "Adi," was the oldest of four children and had left several years earlier. He also lived in Palestine. His girlfriend Maria, who was not Jewish, could not accompany him. She worked as a lab technician in a hospital and kept in touch with Rena and, occasionally, with us.

Adi did not write, nor did he ever telephone. But every few months he would appear, usually after midnight, well-dressed in a stylish business suit, tie, coat and hat, carrying only a briefcase. He was tall, in his late twenties, with light brown hair and hazel eyes, and very good looking. He did not dare to go to Maria's home, but visited Rena or came to our furnished room. He rang the doorbell. As soon as we opened the door he put his index finger across his lips, to make sure we avoided outbursts or the mention of his name.

On these visits, and most of them were very short, he had come from Palestine via Trieste, Italy, or Yugoslavia, traveling on forged documents since it was impossible for a Jew to enter and exit Germany legally. His mission was to organize groups of young Jewish boys and girls, smuggle them out of Germany and ultimately, while evading the watchful eyes of the British Army, into occupied Palestine. The groups consisted of six youngsters and so far no one had been caught by either the Germans or the British. It was a dangerous undertaking to say the least.

During these clandestine visits, he managed to see Maria and she somehow always knew of his impending arrival. She would call us and ask if we had received a "letter" to make sure Adi had shown up.

Maria was tall and slim, had long blond hair and bright blue eyes. She was always well dressed and looked elegant in her high-heeled shoes. I envied her sophistication as only a fifteen-year-old can. It was exactly the way I wanted to look. In the meantime I overheard Maria and Adi making plans for their life together "after the war." Maria had memorized a list of "safe" houses for the children going to Palestine, and Adi relied on her a great deal. Adi once suggested that I come along and join one of his groups to Palestine, but Mother and I were not willing to be separated.

Maria was Adi's secret link to "present-day" Germany. She lived alone, we were not sure where, and she never made mention of her parents or other family members. I often wondered if Adi and Maria were safe. Hardly, I concluded, in spite of the fact that Maria and Adi had a group of friends in the town of Dresden who seemed to help with food stamps and money when needed. We never heard who they were and we had learned not to ask questions.

We did not hear from Maria for several weeks when suddenly our fears became reality. Maria had been arrested late in 1940. She was kept in solitary confinement for three months and then released for lack of evidence. We never found out what the charges against her were. During one of his short visits Adi told us about her arrest, but he was convinced she would never betray him. However, having lived in Hitler's Germany for the past seven years, neither Mother nor I thought that he should or could trust her; after all, she was a German and we had learned to distrust almost all Germans.

"Be careful," my mother admonished him. "You never know what a German will do. We have learned the hard way!" I did not say anything, but I was terrified and convinced if we were caught with Adi, all of us would be shot. Already at an early age I knew enough to be silent: to listen, to see and not to speak. Experience had taught me these lessons. Several of our friends and neighbors had been denounced by Germans to the Gestapo and received long prison terms or were killed outright. Trust in another human being, especially a non-Jewish German, no longer existed.

Adi appeared again in summer of 1941. He brought us greetings from his family, and saw to it that his sister Rena left Germany illegally for Palestine but never divulged how or where he had entered the country, or where he exited German borders with his young charges. We assumed that he must either have important connections in Germany or that his documents were those of a Nazi official or foreign diplomat, but we never found out how he managed to achieve the seemingly impossible. Adi's motto was: "The less you know the safer all of us are!"

Adi and Maria met at night in the basement of various buildings that were now used as air-raid shelters to protect civilians from frequent British bombing attacks. Maria always carried a briefcase similar to Adi's, and I saw them switch cases. During our stay in the air-raid shelter, Adi and Maria always sat in a corner, embraced, kissed and whispered, and the Germans around us smiled benevolently at the lovers.

The last time we saw Maria was August 1941, shortly before we were deported to the Lodz Ghetto. Maria came to our room one last time to see us. Somehow she had managed to hear of our impending deportation, and her informant had given her the date and time. We said our teary good-byes and promised to meet again after the war.

For me, alone and without a single surviving family member, the war ended on April 15, 1945. I tried to make inquiries about Maria in summer and fall of 1945, but I knew so little about her. Had she lived in Hamburg or in Dresden? I never knew; nor had I heard her last name, and I was not sure that Maria was even her real name. How was I to find her? Dresden was now occupied by the Russian Army and it was impossible to even contact the local hospitals to find out if they had had an employee during the war, working in one of the laboratories, named Maria.

Rena and I stayed in touch until her death from cancer many years later. Years before she died, Rena wrote to me from Israel saying that Maria had been killed along with 30,000 other civilians during the 1943 massive Allied bombings of Dresden.

She also wrote that Adi was middle-aged before he married in Israel. She did not seem very close to him and did not volunteer much information other than that he never had children of his own. I would have liked to see him again but he never responded to my attempts to contact him. He became a career officer in the army and died of natural causes at age sixty-six.

Maria's love, courage and daring, her dedication, always remained a silent, unspoken secret. Rena did not mention her existence again in spite of the fact that without her heroism, there were many children, now grown adults, who would not have survived the war.

PART 2:

The Lodz Ghetto, Poland

As a child, I had traveled to Poland several times prior to 1941 to visit my mother's family, but I had never seen pre-war Lodz. My first impressions, after arrival at the ghetto, and while walking under guard from the makeshift Marysin train depot into the Balut section, has remained with me all my life.

The train stopped. There was no platform, no station, only the SS guards, and Jewish Ghetto police wearing yellow stars. The sun was strong, the road dusty. The streets were narrow, often unpaved, with sewage running down along the gutters. It was early fall, and the heat was beating down on our shoulders as we dragged ourselves into the ghetto. We begged for water, and a short stop was made near a courtyard that had a water pump. Having no containers, we cupped our hands to catch the water.

The Balut was a small area, surrounded by barbed wire with red-and-white sentry boxes stationed outside the ghetto perimeter. The German guards with shouldered guns marched back and forth, keeping an eye on our every move.

We saw a few ghetto dwellers: poorly dressed, gaunt-looking men and women who paid us little heed. We did not realize that they had seen new arrivals like our group of 1,100 many times before, and that they had endured ghetto life since 1940. We did not know that most of them were working in factories producing goods for the Germans.

From that day, our life in the ghetto was filled with hunger, typhoid, vermin and helplessness. We called a small room, shared with seven others, home for more than three years. Mother died of hunger there. My little sister was deported from there and murdered. The ghetto field in the cemetery has more than 70,000 unmarked graves of Jews who perished from starvation, disease, hangings and suicide. We existed on little food, lots of rumors and hard work. We had no hope for a future.

Mira

Like a criminal returning to the scene of her crime I find myself, for the second and probably last time, in the Balut section of the city of Lodz of my own free will. I had first made this trip back to Lodz fifty years after my imprisonment. Now again, five years later, the past has pulled me back to the former ghetto where I had spent the years of 1941 to 1944, deprived of family, of food, of a normal childhood and teenage years. I had been cast into an alien world full of horror and pain, and I grew up fast in those three years. I learned what it was to suffer. I learned strength, friendship, and endless fear and hunger. The Germans had transplanted us to this forsaken small piece of earth to die. Inside the guarded ghetto of Lodz we worked for the Germans. We were promised food, but the rations barely sustained life. Day by day we died of starvation, of typhus, of dysentery, and most of us, while still barely alive, suffered from lack of nourishment.

Now, fifty-five years later, tears were streaming down my face. I sat on the stoop in front of the three-story building at 26 Pawia Street where my mother, sister, and I were housed in a small room with four strangers. The building was now occupied by Polish Catholics. Not a single Jew had returned to the building. The names at the entrance downstairs attested to that. I looked, but had not really expected a Jew to live here. Our former individual rooms, one room for about six to ten people, had been consolidated, and the hallways now led to apartments of three or four rooms. The stairway was still filthy, but there seemed to be inside water lines now, although I still saw the outhouse in the overgrown backyard. The building held many memories of friends, women I had known more than fifty years ago. They had taken pity, in their own way, on a seventeen-year-old. They had talked to me, and I had listened. They felt sorry for me, at times even more so than I did for myself. Memories rushed back; I heard their voices, and time stood still. I saw myself, a curious and frightened teenager, lonely and totally alone. I was grateful for their kindness and their friendship, although they were many years my senior. My thoughts, over the years, had often traveled back to 26 Pawia Street.

I dried my eyes, closed them tightly, and the present faded. Memories flooded my mind, and I allowed the waves of memory to submerge me into the past . . .

Walking up to the second floor and I would see the first door at the top of the staircase. The door had a lock and also a huge padlock to protect against intruders. The occupants of that room were Mira and Max

Roizenboim. We exchanged a polite hello in the early days after our arrival, and I watched them unlock the door and remove the padlock. They pushed aside a heavy curtain on the inside and then closed the door. I never could catch a glimpse of the interior of their room and was curious, since I knew by now that these two people occupied an entire small room by themselves without additional tenants. I wondered how they had managed to get permission for that.

I also noticed that the other occupants of 26 Pawia barely greeted them, and usually walked at a distance around the Roizenboims. They shunned them and I wondered why. No one made mention of them and I did not feel courageous enough to ask. After all, I was the newcomer.

The Roizenboims were in their mid-thirties. Max was tall and very good looking. In the winter he wore a black overcoat, which had turned shabby over the years, but at the neck I noticed a collar of gray lamb fur. He must have been affluent before the war, I thought. The coat was several sizes too large for him, and I took this for a sign that he had lost much weight since living in the ghetto. His face was pleasant but gaunt, and he always returned my smile and greeting, sometimes in German, Polish, and even in broken English. He gave the impression of an educated man. He worked in the wood factory and at times brought home a bag of sawdust to help heat the stove. I envied him the sawdust.

Mrs. Roizenboim, or Mira, as I thought of her, was petite, cleanly dressed, and her skirts and blouses, as well as the shoes and boots, told of better times. She occasionally said a few friendly words, and our exchange was in German and Polish. The Roizenboims seemed to be childless and I hardly ever saw anyone come to call, to visit or be sociable. Mira worked in the clothing factory sewing uniforms for the Germans, but never spoke about it.

I often heard her footsteps as she left the house in the evenings after curfew, which was illegal and dangerous if you were caught, and she would return several hours later. It was not until the *Gehsperre*, or total house arrest imposed on the ghetto by the Germans in September 1942, that I finally began to really talk to the Roizenboims.

My sister had been seized by the Germans and deported during the curfew, together with 20,000 ghetto inhabitants. They were never heard from again. The loss of my sister only two months after the death of my mother from starvation made me silent, bereft of all hope, condemned to a life without a future. I had broken a promise to my mother. She had demanded that I take care of Karin, my sister. I had failed to do so. I was not to blame, the Germans were to blame, but I was guilt-ridden and inconsolable nevertheless. Mira was one of those who noticed my despair.

"Why don't you come over tomorrow evening around seven? Since we just received a potato ration, I am inviting you and Moishe Fiszlow to eat with us."

Our ration this time had consisted of three kilos of potatoes per person, a rare strike of good fortune. "I will just have boiled potatoes, but that alone is a feast these days," Mira continued.

I was surprised and pleased and without a minute's hesitation, I accepted her invitation.

Punctually at 7:00 Moishe Fiszlow and I, who was a police officer in the *Sonder Abteilung*, or Special Jewish Police Force, walked from our respective rooms to the Roizenboims. Fiszlow had lost his mother during the Sperre when she, too, was "selected" and picked up with the elderly and taken away. Not even his tears and good connections in the police department had managed to get her released. She, too, had disappeared into the vast unknown that the Germans guarded so carefully.

We knocked on the door. Mira opened it, holding the heavy curtain to the side so that we could enter. For the first time I saw the small room, its furnishings and belongings, and I noticed how spotlessly clean it was. I also noticed a bookshelf with rows of books, most of them in Polish, some in German and English. The bed was made up to look like a couch, and in the center stood a small table with four chairs. Mira had placed four plates, forks and knives on the table and motioned us to sit down. She placed four small potatoes on each plate, and we began to peel, salt and to eat the delicacy, which was to be savored. Each bite was like the most expensive and delicious meal to us. For the moment we seemed content, and the world outside, the barbed wire and the marching steps of the sentry below, had left our thoughts.

Both Max and Mira coughed a great deal. They excused themselves and I saw their haggard, pale faces and wondered what was wrong, but dared not to ask. I walked over to the bookshelf and scanned the titles. What I saw surprised me. Most of the books dealt with religion: Judaism, but for the most part Christianity, the life of Jesus, and similar titles. I was perplexed. After about two hours Fiszlow and I excused ourselves, thanked the couple for the sumptuous meal, and promised to come again, even if there was no food. In our circumstances, lack of food was taken for granted.

I did not see Max or Mira for several weeks and timidly knocked on their door one evening to find out if all was well. Mira came to the door. She wore a long flannel nightgown and had a long, woolen shawl draped over her shoulders. She looked pale and sad, very drawn and tired. "What is wrong?" I asked. Mira motioned for me to come in and sit down.

"I might as well be honest with you. Max and I had tuberculosis before the war and now, without proper nutrition, the old scars flare up. We run a fever now and then, and cough continuously." I offered to help, to bring up an occasional bucket of clean water, dump the dirty water, and try to help. Mira simply shook her head.

"We value your offer. But we manage. We are used to it and we will be back at work soon. We need the midday soup and if we do not work, we do not get the soup."

I nodded my head. "It is none of my business," I responded, "but you should not go out at night. The cold air will do you more harm than good."

Mira nodded. "So you have noticed. I leave here at night, when it is dark outside and when I am well enough I go to the hospital to sit with the sick children. They are alone for the most part, they cry, they have no one. I talk to them, I wipe their foreheads, I sing to them and when they fall asleep, I silently leave and walk back here."

I was speechless. After several minutes I found my voice and asked: "But why you? It is such a long walk from here."

Mira's answer was typical. "Why not? But that is really not an answer. I made a promise to Jesus." I must have looked totally uncomprehending, and Mira continued.

"Max and I met before the war and were married. We never had children because of our tuberculosis. But we shared the same work and the same love for Jesus. We worked at the Mission and believed in conversion just like we had been converted in our younger years from Judaism to Christianity. Max's brother lives in New York and works at one of the larger missions there. If we are lucky enough to survive the war, we will join him there."

I could only nod; I had never heard of these missions but dimly recalled driving with my father through the harbor area of Hamburg and seeing a building with a Hebrew inscription. When I asked what this was, he told me that it was a Christian mission, trying to convert interested and willing Jews. It had completely slipped my mind and I had forgotten about it until this evening. I had never known anyone who had changed religions.

When spring came, Mira coughed less and seemed stronger. She continued to visit the sick at night in the hospital. Once I accompanied her. She read to the children, told jokes, and sang, but never talked about religion. I began to understand why the other occupants of the building shunned the Roizenboims. While they were technically Jews, they had converted and believed in Jesus and Christianity. I was raised an orthodox Jew and did not understand them, but in spite of their beliefs, they were good, caring, and decent human beings. Mira continued her work until the liquidation of the ghetto, when more than 150,000 inhabitants were shipped in cattle cars to Auschwitz. I was on the first transport out of the ghetto, and it took the Germans less than thirty days to complete the total liquidation. A mere 800 went into hiding and were liberated six months later by the advancing Russian Army.

The Roizenboims, like thousands of others, disappeared, and inquiries after the war proved fruitless. The gas chambers of Auschwitz had swallowed them too.

Erika

I was lost and desperately lonely during my second winter behind barbed wire inside the godforsaken place that was Lodz Ghetto. It was brutally cold; frost flowers covered our windowpanes and the icy wind howled without mercy. The heavy, damp snowflakes settled on our heads and eyebrows. It seemed to me that even the elements were punishing us for our unknown sins.

When finally a new food ration was announced and pasted on walls, the ghetto population rushed to the distribution centers, and I was no exception. The lines of people waiting continued around the block into the next street, and I had no choice but to join those already waiting. We knew it would take hours before we would be able to enter the store and receive our meager rations. We stamped our feet, we covered our faces, feeling numb with cold as the wind entered every crevice of our clothing, adding to our misery. But we persisted and the line moved slowly forward, one person at a time. The wait time turned into long hours and my watch told me that I had been standing outside for more than three hours.

Next to me stood a tall, well-dressed woman. I guessed her age to be around fifty. Her cap was pulled down over her ears and only a small strand of yellowish-blond hair showed above the forehead.

During the wait we smiled at each other until finally she spoke, talking to no one in particular.

"The worst possible day to line up and collect the food ration; if we don't die of hunger first, we surely will freeze to death."

It struck me at once: her Polish, like mine, had a heavy German accent and I was curious. "You must have come from Germany originally!" I observed. She nodded.

"Yes, in 1938 from Berlin via the mass deportation to Zbaszyn."

It was getting darker outside and it had become much too cold to talk; swallowing the icy wind was too painful and tore at our lungs. Once our line of anxious ghetto dwellers had moved inside the store, we relaxed a little and the woman, originally from Berlin, now handed me a crumpled scrap of paper.

"This is my address. Drop in some time after work. By the way, my name is Erika Neumark."

I only nodded and put the slip carelessly into my coat pocket. In the weeks that followed I completely forgot about it.

But we were to meet again. One evening, on my way back to the dismal room I shared with six others, I saw her walking with an elderly, frail gentleman on Rybna Street. He was of medium height, thin and gaunt looking but well-dressed, and she held his arm in support. In his right hand he carried a metal "canteen" with a long handle. These were usually used to collect the watery lunchtime soup. We stopped, exchanged pleasantries, and she introduced me to her husband. No first name, just "Judge Neumark." Again I promised to drop by. It was only a short walk from our dismal room on Pawia just around the corner near the barbed wire.

I felt guilty having ignored her invitation, so the following evening I knocked on their door, which had an old yellowing visiting card attached. It read:

"Neumark, Advokat, Berlin."

Erika Neumark answered the knock, opened the door, and motioned for me to enter. She wore a heavy woolen sweater, a dark skirt, and knee-high felt boots. Her hair was dyed yellowish blond (the dye likely purchased through the black market), stylishly set in waves, and pulled to the back of her head. The room, compared to ours, was spacious, well-furnished, and I noticed the German furniture, which I remembered from my parents' home. The wooden floorboards were painted a bright barn red.

Mr. Neumark sat in an armchair, wrapped in a blanket, but the small stove next to him stood cold and idle and no longer gave heat. The bucket next to it no longer held coal or lumber; it was empty. Mrs. Neumark pulled out a chair for me and I sat down. She asked about me, my work, my parents, and where I had come from. Her face looked sad when I told her that my father and mother had been murdered and my little sister deported during the Sperre (curfew) in September 1942.

"We never had children," she said, "and maybe this is for the best now." When Mrs. Neumark heard that we had lived in Hamburg before the war, her face lit up.

"We lived in Berlin and I came to Hamburg frequently to visit friends. It was a different life then, and look at us now!"

She took a large photo album from the table and showed me photographs of herself, her husband and friends. I could hardly recognize them. I saw a tall heavyset woman, elegantly dressed, standing next to Mr. Neumark, who was tall, handsome, smiling and happy. It was difficult to believe that these were the same two people who now sat opposite me. For me it was a sad, quiet visit. Mrs. Neumark kept the conversation going, but her husband sat silently and did not speak. Time passed slowly, and after an hour I excused myself, hungry and exhausted, but I promised to come again.

Weeks passed and I was embarrassed that I had not returned to see the Neumarks. My friend Chawa, who occupied the desk next to mine at the office on Rybna 8, mentioned Judge Neumark. I was curious and she told me all she knew.

"He was a prominent judge here in the ghetto and while details are sketchy, it is common knowledge that he had an argument with Rumkowski [the German-appointed Elder of the ghetto] and he was curtly dismissed from his job, but not before Rumkowski made sure that no one in the ghetto would dare to employ him again."

Curiosity plagued me. I could not imagine that this had really happened, and a few days later I finally decided to visit the Neumarks again.

They were pleased to see me, and Erika was grateful for my company. We made small talk and I finally summoned enough courage to ask:

"I am forward, but I heard talk in the ghetto, and I wonder if I may ask you a question?" Mrs. Neumark nodded her head and I continued: "Is it true that Judge Neumark was dismissed from his job by Rumkowski?" Erika laughed out loud. It was a harsh and pained kind of laugh.

"Yes, it is true," she replied for him. "Rumkowski flew into a fit of rage over a legal decision my husband had made. Rumkowski was meddling in legal matters he did not understand and my husband lost his temper and put him in his place. But it was a short-lived victory. Only hours later Rumkowski sent the Chief of Police, had my husband clear out his office, and escorted him home. He had lost his job, and so did I, although I was only a factory worker. Now we were unemployed and thus also lost the precious noontime soup."

"How do you manage?" I wanted to know.

"Please do not repeat this," Mrs. Neumark pleaded, "but with the help of friends at the lumber factory, our names appear on the roster, which is of course totally illegal. For the time being we pick up our noontime soup. But should Rumkowski find out, it is prison for us, for our friends, or even deportation. We have to be very, very careful."

I was shocked and wanted to change the subject.

"Tell me about your life before the war, tell me about Berlin in those times," I pleaded.

Erika's face lit up and she looked happy. "We had a good life. A comfortable house, servants, and good friends. My husband had a successful law practice. Life was good until 1933, when Hitler seized power. The discriminations against Jews were horrible. You see, I am not Jewish. When I married my husband this had not been an issue, but suddenly it was. I would never have considered leaving him or divorcing him. For me this was out of the question. My family was displeased and angry and in the years that followed no longer talked to me."

"My husband closed his office in 1937. We had enough money to live in comfort, or so we thought. But then, in October 1938, the Germans arrested us and pushed us over the Polish border into Zbaszyn. My husband had been born in Poland, came to Germany in 1920, and got his law degree there. He was never naturalized and had remained a Polish citizen.

"Once we realized that there would be no chance for us to return to Berlin, we had our furniture and other belongings shipped to Poland, rented an apartment in Lodz, and were almost content. But it was a totally different life than it had been in Berlin, more primitive, less affluent and comfortable.

"But peace of mind was not to be. In September 1939 German troops invaded Poland and subsequently occupied the country. Within a year, we and all other Jews were forced into ghettos, into slums, with just our bare necessities. Here we are, as you see us now!"

Judge Neumark had fallen asleep in his chair, and I excused myself and left. After that time, I had seen Erika Neumark and her husband occasionally walking hand in hand, carrying their canteen filled with soup. His walk was slow, his breathing labored, and he had lost a lot of weight. Now, during my infrequent visits, I found Judge Neumark in bed most of the time and I saw Erika alone doing errands, standing in line for food, and picking up the soup. I saw her at the street corner selling some of her scarves, blouses, and other items she no longer needed. The proceeds bought additional food for her ailing and starving husband. She cared for him, she nursed him, and never for a moment left his side. I admired her dedication, her loyalty and above all, her love.

The news that Judge Neumark had died in the winter of 1942 spread through the ghetto and was mentioned in offices, on the street, and in factories. I made one last visit to Erika's ghetto room to express my condolences.

People came and went and there was an endless stream of ghetto dignitaries as well as ordinary folk who had admired Judge Neumark.

Weeks later I met Erika on the street. She embraced me, wished me well, and said: "Please do not listen to gossip and please do not think ill of me."

I had no idea what she was talking about. I could only nod my head. A week later the ghetto grapevine told the true story—the most amazing story I had ever heard.

Erika had decided to leave the ghetto. She did not want to die of hunger now that her husband was gone. She had dressed in her little remaining pre-war finery, applied makeup, had her hair coifed, and walked straight into the red brick building that housed the KRIPO (German criminal police). It was the most feared building in the ghetto. Many had been summoned there, but few had returned alive.

It was said that using her charm, her powers of persuasion, and her flawless German, she pleaded and cajoled until she finally convinced the Germans that she, like them, was a true Aryan and wanted to return to Berlin. She told them her brother was an officer in the Luftwaffe, and in the end she managed to convince the Germans. It was not long before they agreed to her arguments and she was taken out of the ghetto, just one single person, under heavy guard, and supposedly back to Berlin.

It was impossible to believe that Erika had managed to hoodwink the Germans. I now understood her last remark: "Do not think badly of me." She had schemed to leave the ghetto, she no longer had a reason to stay, and maybe she could save herself outside the ghetto. She took just one small bag, and included her photo album.

The room remained untouched for some time. The sign on the door remained "Neumark, Advokat, Berlin," the only reminder of the man she had loved, nursed and cared for to the last moment. After his death, and only then, did she make up her mind to try to survive in Germany. His unmarked grave remained in the ghetto cemetery at Marysin.

I often thought about her, and hoped that she found a good life, an easier life, without hunger, without deportations and without death.

She died in Berlin after the war of old age.

Ruda

Everyone called her Ruda, "the redhead." We did not know her proper first name nor her family name. She was in her early thirties, friendly and cheerful, but her words of greeting were rarely reciprocated. I wondered why she was ignored. She was a slim, blue-eyed, freckle-faced woman of medium height, who had a shock of tightly curled hair. Neither a brush nor a comb ever managed to pass through this strawberry-red tangle with ease.

Frequently, she would sit on the front stoop near the water pump trying to exchange confidences with anyone willing to listen. She seemed lonely and craved company.

"Did you know that I was engaged to be married? I bet you didn't! My betrothed left for Warsaw at the beginning of the war and when the ghetto was closed, he was unable to return."

No one paid attention, no one responded. As a rule she was poorly dressed but occasionally she put on her finery: a black coat covered with lint particles and a black, triangular hat. Rumor had it that she worked in the metal factory, and nasty tongues accused her of having been, or of still being, a prostitute.

She lived in the attic apartment of our building with her fifteen-year-old brother. The attic was unfinished, and the ceiling and walls showed open wooden beams and worm-eaten studs. There were two beds, a chest and an iron stove, but little else. Some clothing was hanging on rusty nails against the walls. There was no linen on the beds, just dirty mattresses with torn covers. The stench in the room was beyond belief.

At times Ruda's brother was seen wearing garments of an orthodox Jew, a long, soiled, dark gray capote, a large hat, and worn, torn boots. He was sullen and totally unresponsive to even a casual hello. Some days he would go to work at the same metal factory, but more often than not, he stayed in bed.

Ruda called him Motek, and her voice reverberated throughout the building when she scolded him. Weeks passed and we suddenly stopped seeing him.

Ruda was again sitting on the front door stoop crying. We listened to her sad story.

"Motek has been sick for weeks now. He was in the hospital and when they sent him home, they placed him in a body cast from his knees to his neck. He has to remain in this position and in bed for weeks, maybe months. It is now up to me to feed him, to clean him, and to take care of him. We have no parents, no relatives and he suffers from a serious bone disease."

We never found out just exactly what was wrong with him.

We finally dared to go up to the attic. We saw Motek in bed. The cast was soiled and so was his bed. When he saw his sister, he yelled:

"It is about time that you come to feed me!" Ruda gave him whatever little food she could. He cursed her for his bad luck, for his misery and for his hunger. She cried wordlessly while she moved about.

Never in my entire life had I seen such squalor.

In fall, the Germans imposed a general ghetto curfew, from September 5 to September 12, 1942. No one was permitted to leave the building. My twelve-year-old sister was at risk of being deported; so were the elderly and the sick, and especially Ruda's brother. Everyone was at a loss. We hoped against hope for a miracle.

Finally, the Germans came with their trucks and dogs and we lined up for inspection. Then, suddenly I saw them. Ruda in her black, lint-covered coat wearing her hat, although it was hot outside. Motek was standing next to her. She had somehow managed to remove his clay body cast and he seemed to be moving about effortlessly, but there was a stiffness to his walk. Now, she looked straight ahead, not at her brother. We could see anger in her eyes, and her fists were clenched at her sides.

My little sister was taken away, but Ruda and Motek escaped the dreaded selection and deportation. Someone asked Ruda: "What about Motek's cast, or his ability to walk?"

"All a fake," Ruda replied angrily, choking back tears. She went to the attic and came back into the courtyard alone, carrying a large, worn cloth bag, and she kept on walking. She did not look at anyone, nor did she speak or respond to our warnings that the German curfew was still in effect. No one dared go outside for fear of the roundup or of being taken away by the Germans and pushed into their trucks. Motek did not accompany her. It seemed to us that she wanted to get away from her brother at any cost. He had abused her for so long. No one knew where she went, and although the ghetto was small, we never saw her again. She no longer showed up for work at the metal factory, and her disappearance remained a mystery. We could only assume that the Germans had seen her on the street and had taken her away on one of their trucks together with the other deportees. It seemed to us that this was what she had wanted. Life had become unbearable.

Motek stayed in the attic, alone and angry, until August 1944. He was seen now and then, sullen, clad in filthy, torn rags and totally unresponsive.

Like all of us, he too, ultimately came to Auschwitz after the liquidation of the ghetto, and there his trail ended. Smoke was all that was left of the life of a brother and sister.

Fajga

In 1942, when I lost my job with the Ghetto Improvement Office because Rumkowski, the German-appointed, Jewish head of the ghetto decided, and rightfully so, that the job was a useless effort, my boss, engineer Adolf Goetz, made several contacts for me. He found me employment in the dress factory. Adolf Goetz had originally come with us from Hamburg. He was an old and broken man, and died of hunger just a few weeks after helping me find a job.

It was almost a two-hour walk to the end of the ghetto where the dress factory was located, and the daily soup was watery and tasted disgusting. But hunger made us eat anything. It was fall now and the walk in the early morning hours was difficult when the wind blew through my thin winter coat. What was I to wear in winter? I wondered.

Fajga and her friend Icek each operated one of the old-fashioned sewing machines in the factory, as they had been doing years before the war. Fajga was about twenty-five years old, plainly dressed, her hair pulled to the back of her head. She had a raspy, harsh voice. Her friend Icek was tall, skinny and slightly bent over. He could have been the same age, or he could have been older; there was no telling.

"Girls, fellows, what we need to do is organize and then strike!" We listened to Fajga's words in stunned silence until someone timidly asked: "Here in the ghetto?"

"Of course!" was her reply. "Where else?" Fajga's Polish was plain and her words direct and without embellishments.

"We have to demand more food for our work. We have to let Rumkowski know that hard work without food is not acceptable! He will have to deal with the Germans on our behalf."

It sounded so simple and logical to us, and during lunch break we walked around the courtyard, shouting: "Bread for the workers, we need bread. No bread, no work!"

After the short lunch break we sat again at our machines, as hungry as before. The following morning the factory entrance was guarded by the Jewish Ghetto police. They warned us in no uncertain terms: "No more demonstrations, no work stoppages, no assemblies, or Rumkowski will take stern actions."

But at lunch break Fajga and her friend again organized a group of about thirty workers and we marched around the courtyard repeating yesterday's slogans.

"No bread, no work, no bread, no work!"

Within minutes the Jewish Ghetto policemen surrounded Fajga, beat her, and took her away. Meekly we returned to our machines and to work.

It was about a week before Fajga returned to work. Her face was bruised and she had spent time in the ghetto jail, where Rumkowski had sent one of his officials to warn her to cease and desist, or else.

But Fajga was determined and obviously fearless. We were afraid and refused to join her. Alone, she marched around the courtyard shouting: "No bread, no work!" Again Fajga was beaten to the ground by the Jewish police with the nightsticks, which they carried in lieu of guns. And again Fajga was taken to prison. This time she returned to work four days later, quiet, subdued and broken in spirit and in body.

My work came to an end at the factory a few weeks later when I was fortunate enough to find employment in an office.

Rumors in the ghetto spread fast and we heard that Fajga would be deported unless her activities stopped. Fajga took the threat seriously and no longer demonstrated. Even she could be intimidated. But during the September 1942 deportation Fajga was picked up by a *sonder* (special Jewish police corps) and put on one of the German trucks. She disappeared along with about 20,000 other ghetto occupants. Their final destination we found out years after the war: The mass graves in Chelmno.

Miriam and Rebecca

The crowded rooms at 26 Pawia Street in the Lodz ghetto made life a living hell. The fights, the complaints and the stolen food supplies forced me to look for another room.

After weeks of searching, I was fortunate to find a room large enough for a bed, a small wardrobe, and a tiny, round iron stove. Moving from one part of the ghetto to another was no easy feat, but Lolek, a young co-worker of mine, found a pushcart and helped me carry my few belongings down to the street. We loaded the cart, pushed it to Lutomierska No. 40, then carried everything to the second floor. It was not an easy move and I was not much help, but with Lolek's assistance, I was able to move in by evening. I could only thank him profusely, for I had no food or money to give him. At last, I had a space of my own; what I had longed for was now mine.

Only too soon it became evident that the room had just a thin plywood wall separating my living area from an adjacent, larger room. The voices of a man, a woman and a child were loud and clear: a constant reminder of crowded ghetto life. It was weeks before I actually met them, or even saw them.

Rebecca, the mother, was in her thirties, gaunt and drawn with a pale face and a furtive look. Her eyes darted back and forth and were filled with fear and worry. She did not even respond to my friendly greeting.

Salek, the father, was about the same age, and was morose and equally unresponsive to my greetings. He was an angry man, as was revealed when his shouted curses traveled through the flimsy wall between our rooms. There were words of reproach, of hunger and hopelessness. The thin plywood hid nothing, not even Rebecca's tears and cries.

Little five-year-old Miriam was a whiny child. Her dresses were torn and soiled. She was emaciated and scrawny looking, had thin matchstick legs and stringy blond hair; she had a large head for her tiny body, and squinty, watery blue eyes. She was a pitiful sight and probably one of the few children I ever considered ugly.

Day and night her voice penetrated the wall. She was either whining continuously, or crying in a soft, heartbroken way. It seemed that she was left alone during the daytime, locked up, and only saw her parents in the evenings when they came home from work tired and hungry. One morning, I left a small piece of bread at their door. But no one made mention of it. It had disappeared by evening when I returned from work. This child had never tasted milk, an egg, an orange or a banana, and whatever food she did receive was hardly enough to still her hunger. The ghetto did not provide for even the most basic needs, much less any luxuries.

The mother guarded her carefully, but at one chance meeting on the stairway she told me more about their lives:

"During the Sperre [lockdown] in September 1942, I managed to hide Miriam. The Germans had come into the ghetto with trucks, dogs and guns and searched for the old and the young and had taken them away. Only a few had managed to stay in hiding and to survive the week of terror.

"I had taken my four-year-old Miriam to the roof of the building, behind the large chimney. I told Miriam over and over again to remain invisible and noiseless, and in the end she must have understood. She stayed in hiding for more than three hours. When the Germans moved on to the next house, I went up and brought Miriam back into the room. She had sensed my fear, and I still find it hard to believe that a four-year-old could have so much sense."

Occasionally Rebecca's remarks were threatening when she wanted to discipline the child. She would say: "The Germans will come." Miriam would become utterly quiet. It was a horrible threat made by a mother at the end of her wits. One could only shudder.

Miriam was a child unlike any other I'd known. She looked at the world from behind her mother's skirt, distrustfully, watching every move. No one could pick her up, and she refused to talk to anyone but her parents. She was not only deprived of food, but also of a normal, innocent childhood, and above all, of laughter. She had never known how to laugh.

The order for evacuation of the ghetto in fall of 1944 took those in the ghetto by surprise. I decided to leave with the first transport. Rebecca, Salek, and Miriam also reported to the rail siding and took the first cattle cars out of the ghetto. They were part of our group. The endless ride in stuffy, hot cattle cars left all of us exhausted. Miriam whimpered; there was no water for anyone, and none to give her.

When the doors finally thrust open the SS shouted their commands. "Auschwitz, line up, and wait!" Auschwitz? No one in Lodz had ever heard of this place. Rebecca carried Miriam. Within minutes men were separated from women, and Salek was marched off into the distance.

Rebecca put Miriam down. They stood quietly in front of me, holding hands. The SS proceeded to separate the old from the young and the children from their mothers. Rebecca's turn came. The SS man yanked Miriam's arm roughly and she screamed. Miriam's horrible shrill sound pierced the air, but Rebecca would not release her child's hand. A man in the SS pointed a gun at Rebecca, but neither she nor Miriam flinched. In disgust, he gave up the struggle, shouldered his gun, and pushed both to the right. He shouted his frustrations, and his words to the two of them cut through the eerie silence: "Verdamt, dann geht zusammen; da ist genug Gas fuer Euch beide."

Damn you! Stay together! There is enough gas for the two of you.

PART 3:

Extermination Camp Auschwitz

(Birkenau)

Auschwitz—the most remembered and talked about extermination camp: gas chambers; crematorium; Dr. Mengele and inhuman medical experiments. Words fail to describe this place. It has been told, written and filmed; yet there is no language adequate enough to tell . . .

Alice

Alice was in our group in the fall of 1944 when we arrived at Birkenau in Auschwitz. She too had come into the ghetto from Vienna and had worked in one of the factories. Alice was a small, mouselike creature, and could have been thirty or fifty. It was impossible to tell. She never mentioned a family member; in fact, she rarely spoke to anyone.

After we had passed inspection, the shaving of hair, and the so-called showers, we were thrown a single rag to wear, but it was Alice who by chance was also thrown a pair of large, wooden clogs, similar to those worn by the Dutch in Holland. While they were much too large for her, it was still better than walking barefoot, as most of us did, during our stay in Birkenau.

In the evening, sometimes early, sometimes late, soup, which consisted of lukewarm water and an occasional turnip, was brought into the barracks in large metal milk cans. We did not have any kind of container, bowl or plate for the evening meal, so most of us used our cupped hands to receive a ladle of soup, which then dripped through our fingers onto the floor.

It was Alice who came to our rescue. She took off her two wooden clogs so that we could use them as "containers" to be filled with soup. After we had hungrily gulped down the liquid and the two shoes were empty, we passed them along to the next two women in line. We all made sure that we kept the shoes in sight and that they were not stolen. We did not think about eating out of dirty clogs, or about what we had swallowed to still our hunger. Once the cans were empty and carried out of the barracks, Alice matter-of-factly put the clogs back on her feet.

This procedure was repeated day after day, week after week, until one morning when we were ordered to remove our rags and line up naked for inspection. Dr. Mengele and two SS officers stood in the center of the Appellplatz to inspect our group.

In Mengele's right hand was a riding whip, and while we each ran past him, he motioned for us to go either right or left, thus separating the weak and ailing from the younger and abler women. Alice, still wearing her clogs, was just ahead of me and was motioned to the opposite side of me. It took just minutes before she and others in her group were marched off into the distance. We watched her go, envying her shoes as our own sore, bare feet were cut and bruised. How we wished for shoes, or boots, or even wooden clogs to ease the pain.

A few minutes later, after we put our rags back on, all 497 of us were herded along a path, past the barracks and into waiting cattle cars. Our long journey in stuffy and crowded cars had begun. It was whispered that our destination might be Germany and a slave labor camp.

Alice and those with her disappeared forever. The gas chambers and crematoria of Auschwitz were working day and night, and now they swallowed another of our comrades.

PHOTOS

Concentration Camp Bergen–Belsen, April 1945 (after liberation).

United States Holocaust Memorial Museum, courtesy of Lev Sviridov.

Women survivors of the Bergen–Belsen concentration camp stand and sit behind the fence of the camp.

Concentration Camp Neuengamme, Dessauer Ufer, Hamburg, 1944–45.

Female survivors lie in bunks inside the barracks of the Bergen–Belsen concentration camp.

Wall sculpture, Elbweg, Hamburg.
Lucille Eichengreen 1995 photo
and poem "Hair".

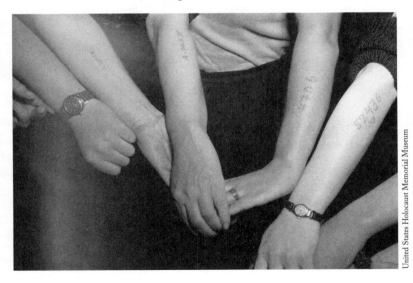

Jewish women liberated from a factory in Mehlteuer display their tattoos.

Jewish deportees from Lodz Ghetto, Poland, arrive in Chelmno, 1942.

View of Bergen–Belsen Concentration Camp from watch tower.

United States Holocaust Memorial Museum, courtesy of Sigmund Baum.

Female Jewish prisoners who have recently been released from Ravensbrueck, cross the Danish border at the Padborg station on their way to Sweden.

Bergen–Belson Concentration Camp, April 18, 1945.

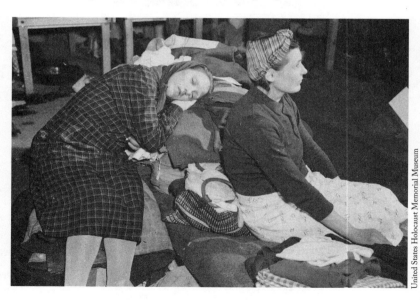

Female survivors rest in the Ernst Leitz Optical works in Wetzlar after their liberation by American troops with the First Army.

United States Holocaust Memorial Museum

Pawia Street, Lodz Ghetto, 1941–1944.

A young woman holds a baby wrapped in a blanket in the Rivesaltes internment camp.

Author at Bergen–Belson, 2010.

Mass graves in distance, 2010.

Author at Begen–Belsen memorial, 2010.

Author has conversation with a French lady who was in Bergen–Belsen sixty-five years ago.

Author reads Yiddish and English comments, April 2010, at Bergen-Belsen.

PART 4:

Concentration Camp Neuengamme

Dessauer Ufer and Sasel

We arrived in fall of 1944 at the outer harbor of Hamburg, specifically in the old storage buildings of Dessauer Ufer. The brick building on the outside looked solid, but once inside we found only bare floors, wooden ceilings and neither cots nor straw for the night. We were marched off daily to perform manual labor on various construction sites like Blom & Foss shipyards, Deutsche Werft and others. It was hard physical labor, with very little food, and we suffered from the cold and rain while the well-clad SS guards found new ways to torment and punish us for not working fast enough. It seemed to me that I had returned after three years to a place I had known so well, but there was no advantage to being here. Escape was still impossible.

Dr. Gisa

We had just been brought to the work camp, Sasel, a satellite of the concentration camp Neuengamme. Our group of 497 women, aged sixteen to sixty, were housed in unheated barracks and had to perform ten hours of slave labor daily on various building sites in and around the city of Hamburg, throughout the winter of 1944–1945. We worked in shipyards and bombed-out buildings using our bare hands as tools. We had no protective clothing to shield us against the cold or snow. We suffered from colds, and bronchitis—some of us were spitting blood—but there was no help or relief.

A small, empty barracks building in the compound was to be used as an infirmary. There was no doctor and moreover, we did not dare afford ourselves the luxury of being sick. So why the infirmary?

During our third week in Sasel, a small woman in a blue-and-gray striped prison dress was brought into camp, accompanied by two SS men. She was thin, but unlike our group, had short blond hair which had turned dark at the roots. Her eyes darted from right to left, and because her furtive looks accompanied her every move, she always seemed like a terrified animal. She took fast, small steps, and was in a constant slow run. She was unable to move in a normal way. We were told that this was Dr. Gisa.

She spent her days and nights in the infirmary with an older woman called Hanka who had been a nurse's aide in the Lodz Ghetto. The Germans had assigned Hanka to aid the doctor as the camp nurse.

Occasionally a medical corpsman from Neuengamme would appear, inspect the infirmary and leave again. He insisted on being called "Herr Doktor."

Only few of our 497 women dared to pay the doctor a visit. We had learned in Auschwitz that sick women were not tolerated, and we were deathly afraid. We remembered those who had been killed because they were not fit for work. Dr. Gisa had no instruments, no medications, no bandages, only strips of paper to wrap around our cut and bruised hands. She could not treat our coughs, or our fever, or our dysentery, and so we still dragged ourselves to the building sites and continued to work.

During the day, while Dr. Gisa stayed in the infirmary, I kept various records in the camp office. Part of my duty was to go to the infirmary once a day to see how many sick had reported as too ill to work. As a rule, very, very few, or none at all were in the infirmary. Gisa and I wanted to talk, but we had to be very careful and spoke in German or Yiddish; but these were short, stolen moments. We decided to meet in the latrine once a day for a few minutes to continue our talks. I knew nothing of her past and was curious to hear what she had to tell. We were on our guard and in constant fear of Germans approaching. There were no locks on the latrine doors, and a German inspection was customary.

In bits and pieces, Dr. Gisa told me her story:

"I was born in Hungary in 1910. I come from a deeply religious family. I had a good education and by 1944 I was a qualified gynecologist. I fell in love with a wonderful man and was married. We had a daughter and were content.

"My life changed suddenly in March 1944, when the Germans rounded up the Jews in my town. My daughter was just three years old and I had barely enough time to manage and arrange for her to be sent to the home of non-Jews. My husband, my parents and I were arrested and sent to Auschwitz, where I lost track of all of them.

"Foolishly, I thought I would tell the block Kapo that I was a doctor and would like to work. Days later I was sent to the camp hospital and assigned to work for Dr. Mengele.

"In Auschwitz the greatest crime for a woman was to be pregnant. I was one of five doctors and four nurses and how I regretted to have mentioned my profession." The words gushed out of her mouth.

"The doctor of death, we called Dr. Mengele. He would perform inhumane experiments on pregnant women, on twins and on the handicapped. He alone decided who was to live and who was sent to the gas chamber."

I was shocked. I had not really known, although I had heard rumors. When we met again the following day, she continued.

"I was ordered by the monster to report all pregnant women in camp. His only aim was to use them for medical experiments and in the end the mothers and the babies were killed.

"I decided then: if I could only help and if it were in my power, there would be no pregnant women in Auschwitz."

Gisa cried, the tears choking her. "I interrupted many of these pregnancies at night, on a dirty floor, with only my filthy hands as instruments. The mothers survived, but you will never know the guilt I feel and price I pay as a human being and as a doctor."

We sat in the latrine, our heads between our knees, talking in barely audible whispers, and crying. Dr. Gisa was shaken as she recounted the previous months in Auschwitz and the fear that never left her.

The women in our camp seldom consulted Dr. Gisa. But during the months that followed, one of our girls became pregnant. Rumor had it that either an SS assigned to our work site or a German foreman had caused the pregnancy. Dr. Gisa reluctantly agreed that an abortion was the only way. Again, without instruments, without sterile conditions, Dr. Gisa performed the abortion late one night; there was much bleeding, but no rags to staunch the flow, no bandages and no medication. The young woman stayed away from work for two days; the sick list stated that she had bronchitis. But in spite of these conditions, her patient recovered in a few days and we were thankful for it and breathed a sigh of relief. Dr. Gisa now was much respected and trusted. She had helped one of us without questioning.

Suddenly, in the spring, Sasel camp was liquidated and we were shipped to Bergen-Belsen. Disease filled every barracks, and typhus killed the great majority of women. Dead bodies lay unburied throughout the camp, on walkways and in huge pits. We knew our days were numbered.

On April 15, 1945, the British Army occupied the camp. They found 10,000 dead, and another 10,000 died in the weeks that followed. Bulldozers had to be used to bury the dead.

We were rehoused in former army barracks and before too long, most of us went our separate ways in the DP (displaced persons) camp, looking for a future away from Germany.

Many years later, and quite by chance, I met Dr. Gisa in New York. She was practicing in the maternity ward of a hospital. At first, we did not speak of the past. We looked at one another silently, as we both remembered Auschwitz, Sasel and Bergen-Belsen. When she broke the silence, she said: "I deliver full-term babies. I know that after Auschwitz, God owes me these lives; these living, healthy babies."

When Dr. Gisa retired she moved to Israel to be with her daughter and grandchildren and after her death was buried near Tel-Aviv.

Three Czech Women

Four hundred and ninety-seven women had arrived in August 1944 at Neuengamme and the work camps of Dessauer Ufer and Sasel. To our surprise, there was no German-appointed camp Elder, or Kapos. But there were forty-two SS guards, both men and women.

Mirka, a twenty-eight-year-old woman who had come with us from the Lodz Ghetto via Auschwitz, helped with the morning's *Appels* (countdowns), lining us up in rows of fives, and reporting in her halting, limited German or Yiddish to the camp commander. During the weeks that followed, no German questioned her self-appointed supervision and leadership. Mirka was short, always running, with dark eyes and a raspy, harsh voice. She was bright, had good common sense, and dreamed of going to medical school after the war. Her brown eyes darted from corner to corner and her voice reverberated throughout the barracks and the Appellplatz. We in turn had no objections to Mirka's commands or her self-appointed position.

The SS camp commander was a middle-aged man with a wrinkled face and mean-looking, dark beady eyes. Camp Commander Stark had been a gardener somewhere in southern Germany before the war. Now, a feeling of importance and his new SS uniform had turned him into a vindictive beast who enjoyed inflicting pain and took pleasure in hitting us whenever possible. We had bloody legs from the nail heads on the soles of his boots when he kicked us.

We had spent the past four weeks in Sasel camp working at heavy construction during the daylight hours in surrounding areas, being transported by train or trucks. We worked without gloves or warm, protective clothing against the winter's continuous rain.

One early morning, three women entered the camp escorted by two SS guards. The camp commander blared out that they were Czech Jews who would be in charge of our group, and that they would act in accord with the orders of the SS.

Gertrude was almost six feet tall and looked as if she had once been heavy. Her skin now hung loosely on her large-boned body. She was designated by the SS as the "Camp Elder." She had a loud, bellowing voice, and she screamed her commands at us in Czech, which we did not understand. She then reported in good German to the SS. Mirka followed her every step and occasionally managed to translate Gertrude's orders into Polish. We missed Mirka's supervision: she spoke Polish to us, we had begun to know her and there was a certain trust; so far she had not betrayed us.

In contrast to our shaven heads, the Czechs had short-cut hair, whereas we were bald and looked like scarecrows. We envied these three women—they had hair. They were now the SS-designated camp Kapos. It took just a few days before Gertrude confided that she was in her late thirties, and had been an opera singer in her native Prague before having been sent to Auschwitz. We in turn seriously doubted that she had ever been a singer of any importance or significance and made fun of her.

The three Czechs were housed in a separate, smaller barracks building, rather than sharing the larger barracks with us. This "status" gave them an air of superiority. Gertrude stayed at camp during the day, and it was never clear to us just what her function was while we were working on the construction sites, or cleaning SS barracks, or working in the SS office.

Every few weeks, the SS "Herr Doktor"—the medical corpsman—appeared to inspect the infirmary and shouted his instructions at Dr. Gisa, who was terrified of the man and barely managed her whispered *jawohl* ("yes"). Gertrude followed his every step. His coat pockets were bulging. He then disappeared with Gertrude into her barracks behind closed doors. When the SS corpsman reappeared several hours later, he was mellow and smiling, and Gertrude's normally surly face looked friendly. His coat pockets were empty and sagging.

The second Czech, Josefa, was a gaunt, plain-looking woman in her forties, brash and loud. She was tall, slim and unattractive. She made no secret of the fact that she had four ex-husbands, and that the last one was a tall, blond German from Hamburg. Every day she accompanied us to the various work sites, was on friendly terms with the foremen and the German laborers and even with some of the SS men, who seemed kindly disposed toward her. She never made friends with any of "the Polish girls," as she called us. We did not like her, but neither did we mind her.

The third Czech woman was Veronika, the youngest of the three, probably in her twenties. She was plump, had wavy, short blond hair, and a big friendly smile. She was kind to most of us, or at least not mean. She never screamed at us, and of the three we much preferred her.

One night in January 1945, after 2 A.M., it was Veronika who was with Dr. Gisa in the infirmary. We saw candles or flashlights dancing about in the dark of night and we feared that the Germans guarding the camp on the outside would take notice. Hanka, the camp "nurse" who was present in the infirmary, swore us to silence, but she told us in the morning that Veronika had had a secret abortion during the night. With a diagnosis of "pneumonia," Veronika stayed away from work for two days while we worried that the SS would discover the truth. What we knew was dangerous and illegal and was never mentioned again. We suspected that the pregnancy had come about on one of the construction sites.

In spring 1945 all of us were again transported like cattle to Bergen-Belsen. We were housed in one large barracks and the three Czechs disappeared into one of the adjacent barracks occupied by Czech women. We did not see them again.

Women in the SS

For a mere 497 sick and starving women with shaven heads and clad in rags, there were forty-two SS guards at Neuengamme and the work camp, Sasel. The guards ranged in age from twenty-one to forty-five, and fourteen of them were women.

Kristie, at twenty-one, was the youngest of them. A petite blonde with a fashionable haircut, she dared to wear makeup, albeit discreetly applied. Her uniform was always clean and pressed, and on occasion she requested a seamstress to shorten her skirts. Her shiny black boots seemed out of place on such a tiny person.

Sophie, a young Jewish attorney by education, had spent the previous four years in the ghetto, and was in our transport from Auschwitz to the slave labor camps. Both of us could speak German, and we were selected for work in the camp office for a short period in the fall of 1944.

Kristie would enter the office, ignoring Sophie and me, sit down at the vacant desk, and unlock the security lock on the telephone. I overheard bits and pieces of her side of the conversation with the party at the other end. I gathered that she had finished high school and did not have to work for a living. I overheard that she had been drafted into the SS and it would have been dangerous had she dared to refuse service. She seemed to come from an affluent family and had many young friends. She often talked of American music and, although forbidden in Germany, she especially liked the Andrew Sisters. Fragments of her conversation—and I only heard her comments and responses—made me believe that she wanted to get out of the SS. In whispered tones she implored her friends to use their influence, to pull all available strings, to try to terminate her work at the camp. She seemed intimidated and was afraid to be a member of the SS. I wondered if she was thinking of the future. Would membership in the SS be a dangerous reference someday?

Kristie never spoke to us. She might have been afraid, or our shaven heads and ragged clothing were too repulsive to her.

The week after New Year 1945, Kristie disappeared. She no longer worked the various shifts guarding us, she no longer slept in the SS barracks, and we did not see her at the telephone in the office. Kristie simply was no longer there. Camp rumor had it that she was on indefinite sick leave. But we were never sure. During the months that followed she did not return and I was happy for her. I wondered how had she managed this.

Two other SS women caught my eye and I had a chance to observe them; they were Elisabeth Robert and Elisabeth Mullen. Both were in their mid-thirties, and both were married and childless. Both were anxiously awaiting news from their husbands fighting somewhere on the Russian front. But otherwise they were exact opposites in appearance and in character.

Elisabeth Mullen was short, stout, slightly cross-eyed and with a permanent that made her blond hair into a frizzy mop. The oblong SS cap she wore could not hide her ugly hair. Her uniform was too tight and ill-fitting for her ample figure. Her skirts were short, and she looked ridiculous in her high, black boots. She had a mean and vicious streak in her personality and a loud and cruel way of laughing. She carried a stick, and took great pleasure in torturing us and calling us vile names.

When one of us was selected to clean the barracks she and five other SS women occupied, she would find fault with anything and everything we did. The floor was not scrubbed enough, the windowsills were not dusted correctly, and the toilet bowl was not snowy white. All work had to be repeated under her watchful eye, with frequent slaps across our faces. The toilet bowl had to be scrubbed with a toothbrush, something we would have loved to have to finally clean our teeth. In the end, hours later, we were dismissed and literally kicked out the door.

One morning, about February 1945, Elisabeth Mullen stormed into camp hitting all who crossed her path. Her fury was boundless. On her left sleeve she wore a black armband. She cursed us without end, shouting "You filthy Jews are at fault that my husband was killed in Russia!"

Her tirade lasted weeks and if at all possible, we tried to stay out of her path. The months that followed did not mellow Elisabeth Mullen; on the contrary, she grew more vile. We wished for her death, but she remained a loyal SS woman to the end.

Elisabeth Robert was another SS woman who came to the office to use the telephone, and during the morning Appel, she would take down numbers of the sick, of those going out on work detail, and those selected to clean up at the camp.

Elisabeth Robert was a tall, fairly slim and plain-looking woman. Her demeanor was businesslike. We never quite knew what she thought of us or if she willingly served in the SS. We did not particularly like her, but then we did not personally dislike her either. She did not beat us, but yelled at us frequently to show her authority. We had no words or personal exchanges, so I was surprised when, one day, she pushed a small toothbrush and a substitute for toothpowder across my desk and walked away. I wanted to thank her, but she only shook her head and kept on walking. The incident was not repeated and neither did we manage to talk. Fear was all around us.

The SS women had husbands in the service of the Fatherland, and Elisabeth Robert was no exception. Gradually we gathered pieces of information to put bits of her life together. She had finished high school, she had worked in an office, and had very poor elderly parents.

To ease his work load the camp commander of our camp selected a "second in command," a tall, good-looking man in his early forties. He wore a wedding band and we assumed that he was married. Walter was infatuated with Elisabeth Robert, and she with him. It was not long before we noticed that they took off together during weekends and returned early Monday morning. This relationship continued during our entire time in Sasel. The fact that both were married to others did not seem to matter.

Elisabeth Robert had ordered Hela, a young woman with whom I had shared an office in the Lodz Ghetto two years earlier, to clean the barracks. In fact, it looked like she had taken a liking to Hela. Hela was in her early twenties, small and wiry, and went about the work in a smiling, willing way. I often wondered if she received an extra slice of bread, or a kind word, but Hela assured me that this was not the case.

One Monday morning Elisabeth came to the office and ordered me to be ready for a ride to Hamburg to pick up provisions in the camp truck. I sat down in the back of the flatbed and to my surprise Hela was already sitting in one corner, smiling. It was a two-hour ride and Elisabeth drove recklessly through the bombed-out streets of what used to be the suburbs of Hamburg. She finally stopped at a stately building on Rothenbaumchaussee, a once elegant neighborhood. Now the neighborhood was shabby, and the building was one of the few remaining structures on a once busy street. If Elisabeth Robert lives here, I thought, she must be very well off.

Curtly she ordered us out of the truck. She walked ahead and motioned for us to follow. Hela and I walked behind her in our ragged clothing, our shaven heads glistening in the morning sun. Our coats had a long yellow stripe of oil paint across the entire width. We were hideous and identifiable. We entered a building and followed her to the back and down a steep stairway. At the bottom she unlocked a door and we entered the dark living room of a poorly furnished basement flat. Her elderly mother embraced her and motioned for us to enter. Not a word was spoken. We had become used to not speaking unless spoken to and Hela and I just stood dumbfounded, without moving a muscle.

Elisabeth Robert pulled out a chair for me and asked me to sit down. Timidly I did. She then led Hela to an old, worn sofa, and made her lie down and covered her with a blanket. I was touched by her gentleness, and her kindness to Hela, whom I thought she had considered only a camp inmate and a necessary and convenient cleaning woman.

Her mother hesitatingly explained that she had no food to offer us, but for two hours at least we could rest without work or beatings. No pleasantries were exchanged, no questions asked, just silent looks. We understood that we had to keep quiet; any word about this visit would endanger Elisabeth Robert. She sat in the far corner and kept up a running, whispered conversation with her mother.

As quietly as we came, we left again, sitting on the open truck for the ride to the warehouse and the waiting provisions. We arrived at camp late in the afternoon, unloaded the truck, and both Hela and I continued our work at camp. Nothing was mentioned to our friends and no reference was ever made to the trip to Hamburg. We were thankful for the excursion, for two hours of rest, and the act of kindness.

Elisabeth Robert and Elisabeth Mullen—two SS women, working within the same system, yet totally different human beings.

The end of the war in May 1945 found us in Bergen-Belsen. The camp SS personnel who had guarded us in Sasel were arrested and subsequently stood trial. The sentences for the most part were light, except for Elisabeth Mullen's; many testified to her cruelty and beatings and she received the maximum of eight years in prison. By the time the former SS were sent to prison, I was already in New York and never wanted to hear about them again. Years later both of them died of old age and natural causes.

PART 5:

Concentration Camp Bergen–Belsen

Again another camp, and, in the spring of 1945, we were transported by truck and train to a camp near Hannover, Germany. By the thousands, we died from typhus. The bodies were lying on walkways, in barracks, and in huge pits, naked and decaying. Those of us who remained were barely able to drag ourselves around. Food did not reach us and we knew that our days were numbered. No human being could survive these conditions very long . . .

We were fortunate; the British Army occupied the camp on April 15, 1945. They found 17,000 bodies. Another 10,000 souls died in the following months, and we, barely able to comprehend what had happened, only wanted to leave that godforsaken place.

Helga and Vera

Bergen-Belsen in spring of 1945 was overcrowded. The barracks were too small to house the women, and the stench inside was unbearable. Whenever we had the strength, my friend Elli and I would sit outside, leaning our backs against the barracks wall. The women around us looked like the walking dead and it did not take long for us to realize that we probably looked just like them.

The only exception were the women occupying the barracks just opposite ours. They were better dressed than we, better fed, and above all, they still had their hair, although it was cut in a short bob. Sitting outside and having nothing else to do, we observed them, and before long Elli approached one of them. They were, like Elli, Czech Jews and had been deported. Elli talked with them daily and enjoyed being able to again speak her own language. I could only catch a few words, and was sorry not to be able to speak Czech. Elli followed them around, talked to them, and found common ground; I sat on the black earth and observed. We had been gathered from many slave labor camps within Germany, but at Bergen-Belsen the Germans no longer provided even minimal food rations.

The men and women in the SS no longer entered the camp. They were afraid of disease and avoided contact with us at all costs. There was only one exception: a young woman. She was short and stocky; her uniform was immaculate and she wore a small oblong cap on her very short, black hair. She entered the Czech barracks several times a day and frequently in the evenings. She was always alone. She was referred to as "Helga." Watching her day after day was a curious experience and I could not find a single reason for her visits.

Finally, after agonizing weeks, the British Army advanced. They entered the camp with their tanks on April 15, 1945. The German SS guards either capitulated by wearing a white armband and letting the British arrest them, or they ran for their lives.

Early on the morning of April 16, 1945, I saw the SS woman come out of the barracks. She no longer wore her uniform, but a striped prison garment like most of the Czech women. She had her arms around a young Czech girl, Vera, who was tall, blond and very beautiful.

Elli saw my perplexed face. "Lesbians," was her only comment. My feelings were in a state of confusion. Had the SS woman helped the Jewish girl? Was it payback time now?

I never found out. Two days later, the woman in the SS was reported. The British Military Police picked her up, and she was imprisoned while awaiting trial. Had the friendship between Vera and Helga been an arrangement of convenience, or had there been true devotion? In 1945 I was unable to understand these women, although I wished them a happier future.

Eva: New Beginnings

In 1941, within the Lodz Ghetto, Rosa and Sol lived on the ground floor of 26 Pawia Street. They had been married shortly before the outbreak of the war, in 1939. Their little daughter Eva was born early in 1941 within the heavily guarded ghetto, which was surrounded by barbed wire. The baby, just like her mother, had reddish hair and pale, translucent skin.

We loved to look at the baby, dressed in pink and white, her large brown eyes staring at us, but she was an unusually quiet infant.

Winter was harsh, and the sky was gray and overcast most days. The nights left traces of frost and ice. No food rations had been distributed for the past four weeks, and hunger was gnawing at us. When would the new food distribution be announced, we wondered? Our conversations centered on one topic only: food. There was no milk for a baby, there were no vitamins, no eggs and no fruit. In fact, there was nothing that provided nourishment for an infant. Rosa tried to nurse Eva, but was unable to produce enough milk. The little one was quiet and listless. There was no medical help, and the doctors all gave the same diagnosis: "lack of food." The outcome was to be predicted: there were no more miracles in the ghetto, and we had ceased to hope. Eva's little face was pale, and her wide-open eyes were without response. She died one night in her crib; it was December 1941. Rosa and Sol buried their infant in the Jewish cemetery in Marysin. There, too, the ground was covered with ice, and snow blanketed the graves of the ghetto dead. Rosa and Sol returned to their room in silent despair, hungry and frozen to the bone.

Rosa was heartbroken, teary-eyed and withdrawn. She frequently undertook the two-hour walk to the cemetery to visit the grave in spite of a merciless winter and howling winds. She left a small wooden marker and vowed to replace it with a stone marker after the war. Sol did not accompany her. He had become an angry, silent and unapproachable man, and, in some irrational way blamed himself for Eva's death.

"Eva's death is my fault, I was unable to provide for her." Those were his only comments.

In spring of 1942, Sol volunteered for a permanent work detail outside the ghetto in spite of Rosa's tears and pleas not to leave her. He ignored her wishes. He, with about one hundred other young men, left the ghetto. They were "shipped" in cattle cars and we had no idea where these men were taken. Their fate remained a mystery and it seemed that they had disappeared from the face of the earth. Rosa never received a card or letter from him, nor any sign of life.

The years passed. Rosa still occupied the same room but she now shared it with several other women. She worked in the ghetto metal shops, providing goods for the Germans. She was withdrawn, kept to herself and never smiled. Rosa always talked about little Eva, but Sol was never mentioned. He had deserted her, and in her mind he too had joined the dead.

During the ghetto liquidation in fall 1944, Rosa, like all other ghetto residents, was shipped to Auschwitz, and from there to several slave labor camps. It was in Auschwitz that I lost track of her.

Quite by accident I ran into her in May 1945, shortly after liberation in Bergen-Belsen. Rosa was well dressed now and more approachable than she had been in the past.

"Are you looking for Sol, or have you heard from him?" I wanted to know.

"Yes, I heard that he is alive and traveling north from Austria and, with a little luck, we will meet here in Bergen-Belsen."

She sounded hopeful and happy and I was convinced that Sol and Rosa had a future ahead of them, together.

It was fall, probably November 1945, when I saw Rosa again. She was beaming. She was also obviously pregnant.

"Sol and I found each other here in Bergen-Belsen and we decided to stay married, raise a family, and are now hoping for papers to leave here and start a normal way of life. Our existence in a DP (displaced person's) camp is not the way you would want to face each day, but for us, especially with a child coming, it has to be a new start in a free country."

I was fortunate enough to leave Bergen-Belsen for Paris in December 1945. From there I went to New York, and many years passed before I either thought or heard from Rosa again. Mutual friends told me that she and Sol had managed papers for Palestine (later Israel) and were living there with their daughter and two sons. I was happy for her. Hopefully a new family had taken the place of the horrible past.

Twenty-five years after Bergen-Belsen, I received a telephone call from Israel.

"Do you remember me? I'm Rosa! The Lodz Ghetto, and Pawia Street 26!" she blurted out.

"Of course I remember you and Sol!" I replied.

"May I ask you for a favor?" Rosa continued. "My daughter, Eva, who was born in 1946, will be coming to the United States to study. Please meet her, and if she needs help, do what you can?" Rosa pleaded.

"Of course, I promise to do all I can," I replied.

Several weeks later I heard from Eva and we met in Palo Alto, California, and spent a few hours over lunch, then walked around town, and talked. Eva knew bits and pieces of her parents' past and their story, and I filled in the blanks of so many years ago. She also knew that she carried the name of her little sister, who had perished in the ghetto. We talked about her future, her desire to obtain a degree in literature, and ultimately, to teach.

"Did your parents ever return to the cemetery in Marysin?" I wanted to know. "No," Eva replied. "They never did and they were told that the exact grave could not be located with 70,000 ghetto dead."

Eva was a beautiful young woman. She looked much like her mother, and I noticed that she seemed to be driven by her father's fierce determination. She also needed to prove to me who she really was. She pulled her passport from her purse and showed it to me. On the second page, together with her photograph, it stated date of birth, as well as "city and country." The spaces were properly filled in: "Born 1946 in Bergen-Belsen, Germany." The place that used to be a death camp had brought forth new life after the war.

I looked at the passport for a long time and then at the young woman, who was truly a miracle from the past.

Eva returned to Israel after two years in California, then married and had children of her own. Rosa and Sol died in their seventies and were buried in Israel.

Dori Tisch: The Marriage

Late in 1945 I had finally made my way to Paris from the displaced persons camp in Bergen-Belsen; food was still rationed, housing was difficult to find, and I managed to share a tiny room on the third floor of the Jewish Youth Hostel at No. 4 Rue des Rosiers with four girls. All four had come from a small town in Hungary, and from there they had been deported in spring 1944 to Auschwitz, and later to Bergen-Belsen. We had never met before, but I gathered that by some means or other they too had managed to find their way to Paris and had arrived two months before I did.

Among the girls my special friend was Dori, with whom I spoke Yiddish. She was exactly my age, and like all twenty-year-olds, we giggled a lot. She confided that she loved to date "Americans in uniform, as long as they were Jewish," and adored the movies, although she did not understand French. She had never been to a movie in the small town where she had grown up, and a city the size of Paris overwhelmed her. Or as she put it: "Here you have to wear shoes when you go outside." Black curly hair framed her face, and her brown sparkling eyes revealed that she enjoyed life to its fullest. It seemed as if Auschwitz and Bergen-Belsen were just a nightmare of the past. I had never seen another human take so much pleasure in dating, the movies, or an occasional piece of cake as Dori did.

She spoke of going to America. "New York is the place for me; you and I will be there within a year at the latest." I was much less optimistic about managing to emigrate. I had received papers from a friend in New York and even my mother's oldest brother in San Francisco sent a sort of affidavit, which the consulate accepted. In December 1945, there was much paperwork to be settled and I was curious how Dori would manage to enter New York legally. After asking her repeatedly, finally she told me.

"My surname used to be Rosen, not Tisch. In 1935, when I was ten years old, my parents decided to betroth me to a young man, the son of a learned man named Tisch. He was exactly my age, but I had never seen him nor had I met him. I had to go with my parents to the City Hall in our small town and sign some legal documents which would make me the wife of Samuel Tisch. Before the law, and in the eyes of the civil authorities, I was now Mrs. Tisch. My parents explained to me that on my sixteenth birthday there would be a Chupa [a wedding canopy] and a religious wedding ceremony to make me officially, and in accordance with Jewish customs, the wife to Samuel Tisch. I accepted this. All this was taken for granted in our town, and children did not disobey their parents. I did not fully understand the meaning of any of this and life continued in its normal way. I soon forgot about it.

"In 1944 my entire family was rounded up by the Germans, sent to Auschwitz, where everyone perished but me. In 1945 I was sent to Bergen-Belsen where I, like you, was liberated by the British Army, on April 15, 1945.

"Several months after liberation, I received a letter through the Red Cross that a Mr. Samuel Tisch in Williamsburg, New York, was looking for his wife, Dori Rosen-Tisch. It gave my parents' names, the name of our town, and my date of birth. Somehow, dimly, I recalled his name, and the signing of papers at City Hall in 1935. It now seemed that the civil authorities, here as well as in the U.S., considered Samuel Tisch's document legal, and I, as his wife, would be entitled to enter the U.S. as soon as all documents were in order."

I was speechless. I had heard of these arranged marriages, but it was difficult to believe that fun-loving Dori would settle down and marry some unknown, Orthodox person in New York.

I was fortunate to be able to leave Paris in March 1946. Dori had given me strict instructions to go to Williamsburg to meet her future father-in-law and convey her respects.

In summer of 1946 I took the subway to Williamsburg and found the street and house number. The apartment was located in the basement of the building. I knocked. A young woman answered and I explained that I had come from Paris and was bringing regards from Dori. She stepped aside and let me enter.

"Before I let you see my father, I will give you some instructions," she advised me. "Do not shake hands. Stand at a respectful distance, and if his back is turned to you, stand still. Wait until my father speaks to you."

Bewildered. I entered a poorly lit room. Mr. Tisch did not look at me. I could only see a middle-aged man, a *kipah* (yarmulke) on his head, and what seemed to be a long beard and sidelocks. I waited.

"I hear you come from Paris." He addressed me in Yiddish. I nodded. "And you knew Dori?" I nodded again. "Do you know when she is coming?"

"I hope some time later this year," I replied. He thought for a while, shook his head and said, "Thank you." His daughter grabbed my arm, led me out of the room, and I left, still bewildered.

Several months later I received a telephone call. Dori was on the line. "I am in New York! I am getting married to Samuel Tisch and I would like you to come to the wedding." I was delighted. Dori gave me the date, the place, and the time. "One warning though," she added. "Wear a dress with long sleeves and a scarf around your head." I agreed.

The wedding was held in Williamsburg in a large reception hall. The men wore long black capotes (coats), large hats or *stramel* (a fur-rimmed hat) and white socks. The women wore elegant dresses, almost ankle length, and the older, married women wore a *sheitel* (wig) and a scarf. The Orthodox ceremony was dignified, the bride very beautiful, and the groom, serious in his strange attire, as was customary for all Orthodox Jews. There was dancing after the vows, but in two separate groups. Men were dancing in a circle only with other men, and in a small adjacent room, the women were dancing together. I regretted not having a camera, but I doubt that I would have been permitted to take pictures.

I did not hear from Dori for about two or three years. Then I got a telephone call.

"Please come to see me, I am very lonely." I agreed, and Dori gave me her address and instructions for the subway. I found my way to a small, modest apartment in Williamsburg. I hardly recognized Dori. We embraced and looked at each other. Dori looked tired and unhappy. Her curly black hair had been replaced by awkward, brown wig, which looked unbecoming and ugly. She wore a plain house dress and had gained a lot of weight.

We sat down. Finally, I broke the silence and managed: "Tell me about yourself and your husband." It took a while before Dori started to cry and to talk at the same time.

"As you can see, I live the life of an Orthodox, married woman. My husband stands on 48th Street in Manhattan. He carries small packets of diamonds in his vest pocket and sells them on the street among the other dealers. It is a living, but not what I had in mind. I sit at home, I clean, I shop and I cook. We hardly talk, there is nothing to say, we have nothing in common. The marriage had been arranged by our parents before the war, and how can I disobey them now? I am expected to produce a child, but so far I have not been able to become pregnant. If I do not have a child, Samuel will ultimately be forced to divorce me. Jewish law favors the man and there is nothing I can say or do. Even if I wanted to, I could not ask for a divorce. I am a prisoner. Life for me resembles the war years; it is different in that there are no beatings, there is no hunger, but there is so much fear and such unhappiness; and I still am a prisoner."

I held Dori's hand and we sat in silence. Both Dori and I knew that we would not meet again. We lived different lives and had only the past in common. I got up, we embraced, then I took the subway back to Rego Park.

Fifty-five years have passed and I have moved to California. I have often wondered about Dori, but never have had the courage to resume contact or to find out about her.

PART 6:

Return to Hamburg,
Fifty Years Later

It was not an easy decision to return to Germany, or for that matter to the city where I had lived peacefully until I was eight years old. My husband and I decided to accept the official government invitation to Hamburg, and made the trip. Rebuilt with German efficiency and American funds from the Marshall Plan, Hamburg was once again a beautiful city, but the familiar Jewish faces from the past had disappeared.

It was a painful, teary visit. Our families were gone, there was no support, no atonement for the horror, and at night, sleep did not come. The week seemed endless, even though our older son came for three days from Paris to join us. My headaches and stomach pains persisted until we left and finally crossed the border into France.

ANNA: A43217l

More than fifty years passed after the end of the war before I first returned to Germany.

Walking around the Grindel area of Hamburg, formerly the home of many middle-class Jewish families, I did not see a single familiar face, no trace of a Jewish butcher store or bakery. In fact, I did not encounter a single Jewish person. Hamburg, a city of over one million inhabitants, now boasted of having a Jewish population of 1,500 souls. Before the war, there were 20,000 Jews living in and around Hamburg.

Hungry, tired, and depressed, I found a restaurant downtown and sat down at an empty table to order lunch. The lady seated next to me smiled. She looked old and tired, was of small build, heavyset, and she had a shock of dark curly hair. She wore a dark suit and looked well dressed. With much relish, she attacked a large bowl of ice cream topped with heavy cream. Her face showed enjoyment and the calories she consumed were obviously of no concern to her. I envied her recklessness.

My lunch came: an openfaced sandwich and a glass of iced tea.

The room was crowded now with other lunch guests and it was getting stifling hot. I removed my jacket. The lady next to me smiled and removed hers.

"Just too hot," she commented.

My startled glance came to rest on her left arm. I saw a large blue tattoo spelling out "A432171." I shuddered as I recognized the Auschwitz number.

In a city so large, with such a minuscule number of Jews, the probability of sitting next to an Auschwitz survivor was almost nil. (Hamburg's archives listed only two Auschwitz survivors.) I introduced myself. The lady looked startled, almost frightened.

"I too was in Auschwitz in 1944," I managed to stutter. She looked at me in disbelief.

"Really?" she replied, but her voice was filled with doubt.

"Yes, please believe me. I went to school here in Hamburg at Carolinenstrasse before the war."

She seemed to relax and showed some interest.

"Did you know my niece Laura Harness?" she wanted to know.

"I think I recall a classmate in 1938 by that name."

She nodded her head. "Yes, it must be my niece. I am Anna Feldman."

We shook hands and unintentionally, my fingertips traced the number on her arm, "Please tell me about yourself. What happened to you, and how did you survive?"

Anna thought for several minutes before she decided to respond.

"I was born in 1910 in Hamburg and my older brother and I lost our mother when we were very young. My father remarried and I loved my new mother. I came from a very traditional home. Outside the world was anti-Semitic, but I was a free spirit, liked to walk outside, rain or shine. My father was sickly and the financial situation at home became desperate. When I graduated from eighth grade, I decided to help my parents and went to work in a factory. There was much unemployment in those days, and my brother and were happy to have jobs."

Anna was quiet for some time and seemed to think about the past. She stirred the ice cream with her spoon, but did not eat. Then she continued.

"I joined a Jewish youth organization and it was there that I met a young man named Mike. We fell in love, but I found out only too soon that Mike worked as a labor organizer, opposing the new Nazi order. On and off, he was arrested, he was beaten, and then eventually released. During one of those short releases, we were married in a simple religious ceremony. In 1934 he started working for the Resistance, but he was caught again and arrested.

"I was no longer permitted to work and had to live in a furnished room. It was during Mike's arrest that I found out I was pregnant. Mike's trial brought a verdict of two years' hard labor and prison time, and I was alone. We lost many friends; some emigrated, others were killed or tortured and some committed suicide. My little girl was born while Mike was still in prison, and having no means, I had to go to the county hospital where they took care of the indigent and the poor."

Anna rested, and her thoughts seemed in another world. I waited and eventually she continued.

"When Mike was finally released, we began to realize that he had to leave Germany. He was under constant surveillance and in imminent danger. Friends arranged for him to cross the border into Holland and I was again alone with my infant. I enrolled in an art course offered by the Jewish Community Center, and hoped that eventually I would be able to support myself. Being 'on the dole' was painful, and I felt ashamed that I had to accept this kind of help just to eat.

"After Kristallnacht on November 9, 1938, a woman approached me on the street one evening.

"'I have regards for you from Mike,' she said. She was of medium height, plainly dressed and spoke German. 'I also have the necessary papers for you to leave here, and cross the border into Holland. Take your baby tomorrow at six P.M., but very little else, and meet me on this street corner. I will not wait for you if you are not on time. It is too dangerous.'

"I was desperate. Should I trust her? Would she help or betray me? I decided to trust, and within three days, and many detours filled with fear, we arrived in Holland and Mike was waiting for us. I will always recall his words. 'You are here now, you are safe, and nothing can happen to us anymore.'

"We were very poor but received help from local Jewish organizations, a little money, some food and clothing, and somehow we managed. But all this changed drastically in 1940. Holland was invaded by the Germans, and while there was resistance, the country was occupied. We were in constant fear for our lives, and again, we had to live under Nazi laws and terror."

Anna was quiet for a few moments.

"My little daughter found refuge in a home for orphaned children and I joined the Resistance as a courier. Mike and I worked underground, and not a day passed that one of our friends was not arrested and shot. But there was nothing else to do. I missed my little one, but visits were too risky and all I could do was hope and pray. But in 1943, we were denounced and the German secret police arrested us, and this time I, too, found myself in prison. My fears never left me. I feared for my life, for Mike's and for our little daughter."

Anna cried as she spoke.

"After eight months in prison I was brought to a large camp and given to understand that we would be transported east. We were put in barracks, without beds, without cots, and we waited. Cattle car after cattle car left Holland. Our final destination was Auschwitz.

"You have been to Auschwitz. I do not have to tell you about that place, right?"

I nodded my head and replied, "You arrived in Auschwitz a year before I did. Did you work there?"

"Yes, we worked in a factory during the day and were marched back to camp at night. One day in the factory, an SS man asked if any one of us could sew. I raised my hand. The SS man took me to his office and gave me material, yarn and needles, and ordered me to make a doll for his daughter. For a few days, I was in a warm room, I received some food, and finished the doll. Then I was sent back to the factory. You too will recall that we had to undergo periodic inspections, which most of us did not survive. We were thin and sickly and were no longer considered fit for work. Many of my friends did not survive. Auschwitz had a resistance movement, but we were not very effective other than that we supported each other and committed small acts of sabotage."

Anna paused again.

"I recall January 1945. Auschwitz was being evacuated and we were marched for miles without end. Our final stop was Ravensbrück. Here there were no gas chambers. Here you simply died of hunger and disease. In spring 1945 we were on the march again, and were finally liberated by the advancing Russian Army."

Anna's ice cream had melted. She obviously had lost her appetite.

"Slowly and by devious routes I made my way to Holland, on foot, on horse-drawn carriages and occasionally on a train. I had no money. But it was in Holland that I found Mike again. He too had been in various camps and knew that I would look for him in Holland. We looked at each other, neither believing that the other was still alive. Our tears and our embraces made us realize that we still had a life ahead of us.

"With the help of the Jewish Committee we managed to find our little daughter, and a room for the three of us. The family who had taken care of our little child as if she were their own were heartbroken to give her up.

"The Jewish Community supported us and eventually we found work in the Jewish Orphanage, where we worked for five years. In the early fifties the orphanage was shut down, liquidated, and the Dutch government did not grant us work permits. Everyone who had left for Israel wrote us: 'Don't come. Life is hard here and not a place for those who survived the camps.'

"Then in 1952, having no choice, we returned to Hamburg, the place where we were born. We began to live in Germany, received loans from the government, some compensation as well, and started a small business. But whatever we received did not nearly compensate us for the years in concentration camps. Painfully, we learned that anti-Semitism still existed in Germany, but in our lifetime we had learned a lot, and we now learned to adjust and to live in Germany. The German civil service offices and their personnel were, and still are, very accommodating and I should not complain. This is life. One has to make the best of it."

Anna was silent. This was all she wanted to tell. Tears were running down my face. My fingers rested on her Auschwitz number. This woman was eighty-two years old. I admired her strength and her courage and dared not ask more . . .

For Sale (Sold)

Cela and I met for the first time when both of us were fortunate to receive a job in the evening kitchen providing a nighttime meal to deserving workers for a period of two weeks. Rumkowski, the Elder of the Jews of the Lodz Ghetto, had personally selected about twenty young women to work in the kitchen, to wait tables, work in the office, collect coupons. For this we received an additional meal. Cela liked to talk with me. She had a loud, shrill voice, was tall, very good-looking, and had long, blond, wavy hair. When she spoke she had a silly laugh and was shunned by most of the women working with us; they had labeled her as stupid. I listened to her, but could not figure out what she was saying, my Polish and Yiddish both being barely adequate.

After a few weeks, she invited me to come home with her after work. She lived, and had lived before the war, in the Baluty section of Lodz, the poorest area of a large city, occupied by thieves, gangsters and figures of the underworld. Now the area was entirely occupied by

Jews. On German orders the non-Jewish inhabitants had moved away.

We entered the dirty courtyard in the backyard of an old building. Once inside, I was surprised to see an apartment with several rooms, a kitchen, and prewar furniture. My surprise must have shown. The ghetto population usually occupied a single room for six or eight people. "We lived here long before the war. My father conducted his business in this area, and we knew everyone in Baluty."

I was about to ask more questions, such as what kind of business did he have, when Cela's parents entered the living room. Her mother was tall, heavyset, and wore an abundance of necklaces and rings. In contrast, her father was short and heavyset, with a permanent grin on his face. He looked me over carefully, and for no apparent reason, I shivered. He finally spoke: "What did your father do for a living?"

My answer, that he was a vintner, did not impress him. He just murmured "feh" in a disgusting way and motioned us to sit down. There followed many questions concerning my family's money, real estate and other matters, which I could not answer.

He told me that he had three daughters and that he and his family were very well off. Exactly what he was doing for a living he did not say. But he told me, in a bragging way, about his middle daughter, who was not in the ghetto, "In the thirties a man came to town with a great deal of money. He had arrived from Buenos Aires,

Argentina, and intended to return. I only knew that he was Jewish, since we talked in Yiddish. He offered me a great deal of money if I would permit my daughter to return with him to Buenos Aires. She would be working there in a good position and earn a great deal of money. I did not need much time to think about his proposition. He would pay me a good sum right now, and she would be assured of a job in Buenos Aires. We packed her things and she left with him a few days later. One single letter came from her, but nothing else. Then the war broke out, and all mail abroad ceased. We hope to hear from her when the war ends and maybe join her."

I was at a loss for words until I finally managed, "Did you really take money and let her leave the family?"

He nodded his head and Cela just giggled in her usual way. I failed to understand, but the story remained in my mind during the war. After the war, shortly after liberation, I met Cela in Bergen-Belsen. I was still in my camp rags, but Cela was well dressed, did not have shorn hair, and wore lovely leather boots. We looked at each other until I finally managed to say, "How did you survive and look human?" Cela threw her head back and laughed her insane, loud laughter. "Very simple, I lived with the German camp commander, had enough to eat and did not suffer." At a loss for words, I wished her well, and went on my way.

Her father's story remained on my mind and when my sons were grown, more than fifty years later, we took a trip to Buenos Aires. Many questions still bothered me.

I found the address of the Jewish Community offices, and I took along a friend who spoke English and Spanish. We found an elderly lady willing to talk with us. I told her my story. She listened carefully and asked for the name. I gave her Cela's last name; she looked into some old and worn ledgers and asked for the exact year. I did not know.

Finally, she told me the following: "In the thirties it was common practice to pay a family in Poland if they let one of their daughters leave for Argentina. They arrived here and were placed in various bordellos to work. Very few of them managed to escape. The Jewish community despised them. Jewish laws did not permit that they be buried in the Jewish cemetery. Only in the last years has this come to the surface and much has been written about it, but we are unable to find accurate information, except in a couple of instances where the relatives had more details. Much research is yet to be done before we have a clear picture of all the details, names, and where they came from."

She assured me that my story was based on fact and had credibility. We thanked her and left. Cela's silly, disturbing laugh rang in my ears. I know that she is now living in Scandinavia, but I do not have the courage to contact her.

Epilogue

April 15, 1945–April 15, 2010
Concentration Camp Bergen-Belsen, Germany

At the invitation of the director of the Gedenkstaette Bergen-Belsen I found myself on April 15, 2010, standing besides the mass graves of those I loved, those I knew, and those with whom I had shared years of hunger and torture.

The wind today was gentle. I shivered, and tears covered my face.

Sixty-five years after the British Army had occupied this camp, I stood alone, remembering those who had not survived. They had died miserably: of typhus, of hunger, and of pain. Buried in nameless mass graves, thousands of them were left here. They had had hopes of peace, of a life after the war, but it was not to be. And they, like Anne Frank, believed in the goodness of men.

I had a second chance to live and to recall the past. I cannot forget, and I cannot forgive.

Selected Bibliography

Aubrac, Lucie. *Outwitting the Gestapo*. Translated by Konrad Bieber. Lincoln, NE: University of Nebraska Press, 1993.

Bernard, Catherine. "Women Writing the Holocaust." Honors thesis, Stanford University, 1995.

Box, Pascale. "Women and the Holocaust: Analyzing Gender Difference." In *Experience and Expression: Women, the Nazis, and the Holocaust*, edited by Elizabeth Baer and Myrna Goldenberg. Detroit: Wayne State University Press, 2003.

Delbo, Charlotte. *Auschwitz and After*. Translated by Rosette C. Lamont. New Haven, CT: Yale University Press, 1995.

Distel, Barbara, ed. *Frauen im Holocaust*. Gerlingen, Germany: Bleicher, 2001.

Herbermann, Nanda. *The Blessed Abyss: Inmate #6582 in Ravensbrück Concentration Camp for Women*. Translated by Hester Baer. Edited by Hester Baer and Elizabeth Baer. Detroit: Wayne State University Press, 2000.

Hilberg, Raul. *The Destruction of the European Jews*. Rev. ed. 3 vols. New York: Holmes and Meier, 1985.

Isaacson, Judith Magyar. *Seed of Sarah: Memoirs of a Survivor*. Urbana, IL: University of Illinois Press, 1991.

Kaplan, Marion A. *Between Dignity and Despair: Jewish Life in Nazi Germany*. New York: Oxford University Press, 1998.

Katz, Esther, and Joan Miriam Ringelheim, eds. *Proceedings of the Conference on Women Surviving—the Holocaust*. New York: Institute for Research in History, 1983.

Meed, Vladka. *On Both Sides of the Wall*. Translated by Steven Meed. New York: Holocaust Library, 1979.

Millu, Liana. *Smoke Over Birkenau*. Translated by Lynne Sharon Schwartz. Evanston, IL: Northwestern University Press, 1998.

Ofer, Dalia, and Lenore Weitzman, eds. *Women in the Holocaust*. New Haven, CT: Yale University Press, 1998.

Rittner, Carol, and John Roth. *Different Voices: Women and the Holocaust*. New York: Paragon House, 1993.

Roth, John. *Holocaust Politics*. Louisville, KY: Westminster John Knox Press, 2001.

Sutin, Lawrence. *A Postcard Memoir*. St. Paul, MN: Graywolf Press, 2000.

About the Author

Lucille Eichengreen was born Cecilia Landau in 1925, in Hamburg, Germany, of Polish parents. Her father was murdered in Dachau in 1941. Her mother died of hunger in the Lodz Ghetto in 1942, and her sister Karin was murdered in Chelmno in 1942. Lucille survived the Lodz Ghetto, Auschwitz, Neuengamme and Bergen-Belsen between 1941 and 1945.

She published *From Ashes to Life* and *Rumkowski and the Orphans of Lodz*, and has taught at colleges and universities in the United States and Germany since 1991. She received an honorary doctorate from the Justus Liebig University, in Giessen, Germany.

Lucille Eichengreen lives in California as do her two sons, Barry and Martin. Her husband Dan died in 2000.